ReVisionary Thinking

T0017929

*Re*Visionary Thinking

Have to
When You^Change Your Plans
to Reach Your Goals

Courtney Clark

© Copyright 2022–Courtney Clark

All rights reserved. This book is protected by the copyright laws of the United States of America. No part of this publication may be reproduced, stored in or introduced into a retrieval system, or transmitted, in any form or by any means (electronic, mechanical, photocopying, recording or otherwise), without the prior written permission of the publisher. For permissions requests, contact the publisher, addressed "Attention: Permissions Coordinator," at the address below.

Published and distributed by:
SOUND WISDOM
P.O. Box 310
Shippensburg, PA 17257-0310
717-530-2122
info@soundwisdom.com
www.soundwisdom.com

While efforts have been made to verify information contained in this publication, neither the author nor the publisher assumes any responsibility for errors, inaccuracies, or omissions. While this publication is chock-full of useful, practical information; it is not intended to be legal or accounting advice. All readers are advised to seek competent lawyers and accountants to follow laws and regulations that may apply to specific situations. The reader of this publication assumes responsibility for the use of the information. The author and publisher assume no responsibility or liability whatsoever on the behalf of the reader of this publication.

The scanning, uploading and distribution of this publication via the Internet or via any other means without the permission of the publisher is illegal and punishable by law. Please purchase only authorized editions and do not participate in or encourage piracy of copyrightable materials.

ISBN 13 TP: 978-1-64095-369-7
ISBN 13 eBook: 978-1-64095-370-3

For Worldwide Distribution, Printed in the U.S.A.

1 2 3 4 5 6 7 8 / 26 25 24 23 22

This book is dedicated to Jamie.

And to Anthony.

And to our pets.

The family we've made is greater than any family I could have envisioned. Life's funny that way, huh?

Contents

Introduction

The ReVisionary Path

"All human plans [are] subject to ruthless
revision by Nature, or Fate, or whatever one preferred
to call the powers behind the Universe."
—Arthur C. Clarke

*A*llyson Felix was terrified to tell the truth. She knew she would be in trouble when everyone found out, but she needed to keep the secret just a little bit longer. As she laced up her running sneakers, the clock ticked over to 4:30 A.M., like it did every day when she left the house. She headed out into the darkness of the early morning, her feet hitting the pavement.

Felix wasn't just any woman going for a morning run. She was an Olympic athlete with nine medals to her name. She was a world champion and a fierce competitor. But everything was about to change. Because Allyson Felix was going to have a baby.

In 2018, Felix was renegotiating her contract with Nike, where she served as one of the brand's most marketed athletes. She knew, like many women runners before her, that pregnancy and motherhood were often considered career-ending. But she didn't accept that belief. She wanted to be a runner *and* a parent. And she was doing everything in her power to be both.

When Nike found out about Felix's pregnancy, they offered her a contract with a 70 percent pay cut compared to her previous contracts. The performance requirements in the contract stipulated that if Felix didn't perform at her best in the months just before and after giving birth, she could be punished with further financial penalties.

Felix turned them down.

She walked away from her negotiations with Nike and signed a contract with Athleta, becoming that brand's first ever sponsored athlete. She gave birth to her baby daughter and continued to train. Six months after her daughter was born, Felix's opinion piece in *The New York Times* detailing the events of her negotiation with Nike went viral, causing Nike to institute a new maternity policy for women athletes.

But Felix wasn't done yet. She began training for her post-pregnancy comeback at the Tokyo Olympics, undaunted by even the quarantine measures early in the COVID-19 pandemic. Olympic gossip said she was too old and out of practice to perform well at the Olympics. But Felix trained wherever she could: empty soccer fields, beaches, and neighborhood sidewalks. She walked away with a gold and a bronze medal and became the most decorated track and field athlete in Olympic history, even surpassing Carl Lewis.

When Felix had to face losing the most coveted brand sponsorship contract in sports, she changed the narrative. Instead of feeling sorry for herself, she found a contract that worked better for her. Instead of accepting the expectation that motherhood would end her competitive career, she broke Olympic medal records.

How do you make a new plan when your old plan falls apart?

How do you, like Allyson Felix, achieve your goals when the goalposts move on you?

How do you reach success when the path in front of you changes?

You may not realize it, but you've probably done this before. As a child and young adult, you got lots of practice adjusting your behaviors to get what you wanted. You did this when your first crush rejected you. When you didn't make first string or lead role. When you didn't get your first-choice college, or first-choice job, or first-choice house.

But along the way, we often forget how to adapt. As we grow up and get better at the tasks of living—of making our lives fall into place through hard work—we get *worse* at the task of bending. Being flexible enough to adjust our plans gets harder.

This book is a guide for those "what now?" moments in life.

Maybe you've hit a roadblock and need to make a change. Maybe a change is being forced on you against your will and you're struggling to get acclimated. Maybe you survived a global pandemic but the world looks different now and you're trying to find a "new normal."

Within these pages, you'll encounter research, stories, and strategies for becoming more flexible and adaptable in the face of adversity. Even more than positivity, perseverance, or intelligence, scientists are starting to realize that adaptability is a large part of how resilient a person is able to be. The more adaptable you can become, the more likely you'll be able to achieve your goals, even when faced with uncertainty and change.

The Red Pen of Revision

I used to think I was supposed to get everything right on the first try. I admit I was a bit of a teacher's pet, especially in English class. I loved writing, I used big words and flowery language to make my points, and I usually nailed my essays and writing exercises on the first try. I'd never been asked to edit an essay and turn the revisions back in.

Until junior year.

When Mr. Heup handed me my first essay back junior year, the page was covered in red ink. Sixteen-year-old me was mortified! *What in the world could he possibly be criticizing?* I wondered. It didn't seem fair.

When it was my time to talk to him, I stuffed down my annoyance. I pulled out the stapled paper and pointed to the top. "So what?" was written in giant red pen. "Mr. Heup, what does this mean? Why did you write 'So what?'"

He said, "What you wrote was good writing, but it didn't come to any conclusions. You made some comments about the main character, but what does that MEAN? If it's true for her, then what does that mean for other women? For society as a whole? Expand on your point. So what? Why does this matter? How does it relate to what we all experience? Make a bigger comment about life. Make a point."

I went home and started to think. *What DOES it mean?* I wrote, scratched it out, rewrote, and revised that paper not once, not twice, but *three* times to earn my A. For the next two months of class, Mr. Heup would mark my papers with "So what?" until I started asking that question of myself.

Approaching writing assignments with this question in mind enabled me to realize that usually, the initial thoughts I had weren't the whole story. I discovered the value in revisiting my early drafts and evaluating what I had done before. I discovered the power of revision. Sure, small edits could make an individual sentence more powerful, but sometimes what was needed was a more "global" change—a new way of presenting my argument, a new path to purpose.

And something amazing happened: my essays got better every time I rewrote them. Each revision wasn't about doing MORE; it was about going deeper. Mr. Heup and his red pen taught me to be willing to make changes to realize greatness. He taught me that if we don't ask ourselves "So what?" then we just settle for "what is."

If we don't ask ourselves "So what?"
then we just settle for "what is."

We settle for "what is" a lot, don't we? Think about how much language we have that seems to glorify NOT changing:

It is what it is.

That's the way we've always done it.

The devil you know beats the devil you don't.

That won't work here.

That's a whole lot of ways to say: *I'd rather suffer under sameness than change.*

And I get it: It's not JUST that making change is uncomfortable. It's that change ALSO seems to take us further away from something we've been working toward. Something we've been wanting or expecting. It's annoying *and* it's sabotaging. But we can't avoid change completely, so how we handle it matters.

Slippers and Grippers

If handling change sounds daunting, you aren't alone. For two years I conducted research on how people cope under the stress of change. A whopping one in three employees reported to me that they struggle to stay motivated when facing a challenging new problem.[1] It's not just that they don't know what to do in an uncertain and new situation—they're grappling with a sense of discomfort so intense that they'd rather avoid the problem than find the answers.

When things go sideways, most people make one of two mistakes: they either give up on their dreams or they NEVER give up on their dreams.

The people who give up on their dreams too easily say things like "Oh, that wasn't meant to be. I'm not the kind of person who gets to have things like that." They let their dreams slip through their fingers at the slightest bump to avoid disappointment. We'll call them "Slippers."

The ones who refuse to give up on their plans are called "Grippers." Grippers won't let go, even if their plans aren't working. Even if their desires are causing them more pain than pleasure. *What's wrong with that?* you might wonder. *Aren't we supposed to be tenacious and go for what we want?* The answer is...*sort of.* If you insist on grinding toward a goal no matter what happens, you might just grind yourself into dust.

When things change, sometimes you need to shift along with them. It's not that you can't still reach your ultimate goal, but you have to accept that it's going to look different. You can change your plans and still reach your goals. Scratch that. You HAVE to change your plans to reach your goals.

That's the real work of resilience. Resilience isn't superhuman internal strength. It's not toxic positivity. It's not sucking it up when things suck. Real resilience is letting go of the "old way of doing things" and rewriting how you're going to get from where you are to where you're going.

Here's what I've learned: **The success of your vision comes from the REvision.** Your happiness and achievement in life aren't just based on how good your plan was, but on how willing you are to rewrite a new plan when you have to. Rewriting that new plan is called **ReVisionary Thinking.** It's pulling out that red pen and getting to work on what the next draft of your success looks like.

When life is a struggle, you can adapt and still get what you want. Change doesn't have to alter where you're going, but it may shift how you have to get there.

The success of your vision comes from the REvision.

A ReVisionary Plan

Over the course of the book, you're going to meet researchers and regular people who have become experts (sometimes by accident!) in revising their plans. You're going to hear untold stories of wildly successful people who hit a roadblock but still became the big name we all know today. How did they do it?

What these ReVisionary Thinkers have in common is flexibility. Research shows that people who can "think flexibly, produce alternate

15

explanations, reframe positively, and accept challenging situations or distressing events" tend to be more resilient.[2] Cognitive flexibility is a way you can take your experiences and expectations and view them through a lens of possibility. When you're able to see stressful situations as challenges rather than threats, you'll experience less distress and encounter more opportunities for success.[3]

To make a new plan (a GOOD new plan—maybe even better than the old plan!), these ReVisionary Thinkers followed the same framework. Each one moved through three stages: Let Go, Think Up, and finally Move On.

Let Go, which you'll learn about in part 1 of this book, is about the willingness to toss out the way you've always done it. You'll learn about what keeps us from moving on and why some people struggle to let go of "the plan" they have for their life. You'll also learn strategies for confronting the grief that can come from releasing a plan that isn't working anymore. You may be surprised to learn that some common strategies for decision-making are causing you to have a hard time letting go of your plans.

In part 2, you'll challenge yourself to **Think Up** new possibilities for moving forward. This stage of ReVisionary Thinking is the most likely to be skipped over, and yet it is one of the most critical. In this stage, you'll be asked to rethink how you brainstorm and to learn new ways for creating choices. You'll also come to understand why obvious decisions aren't always the best options when it comes to revising your plans.

Finally, part 3 will help you plan what it looks like to **Move On**. How will you decide how to move forward? What does it look like to get smart input from other people, and how do you know whom to listen to?

You don't need fixing—
your plan needs revising.

Every ReVisionary Thinker—and just about every successful person you look up to—has been challenged to revise and be flexible at some point in their lives. They've moved through these three stages, either intentionally or instinctively, to find their way back to success no matter what knocked them off course.

To follow these three stages isn't complicated or time-consuming, but many people just don't bother. They look for shortcuts, easy answers, or "hacks" to avoid having to move through change. Revising your plan is simple, once you understand how. No hacks needed.

When uncertainty rocks your world, it's easy to feel like you need to "fix" yourself. But *you* don't need fixing—your plan needs revising.

PART 1

LET GO

Chapter 1

Your Sticky Life Plan

"We have a plan for life but sometimes,
life has a different plan for us."—Saji Ijiyemi

*A*s young children, many of us learn how to set goals. As we grow, we're taught how to work toward our goals. We're encouraged to put in effort, to try our best, and to never give up.

But we're *not* often taught what happens if life throws a roadblock in our path. We dedicate significant effort to going for the goal, but we spend little time learning strategies for what to do when the goalposts move. With a single-minded commitment to a goal and few skills to adapt, it's no wonder we get frustrated when change happens.

When unexpected situations force us to change our plans, it's human nature to resist that change. Why? Because we created those plans so that we could be successful. We want what we want because we think it's the best way to get where we're going. Life plans tend to feel "sticky" because letting go of them feels like letting go of our goals. But that's not always the case.

In part 1, Let Go, you're going to be challenged to release your grip on your previous expectations, because an inability to shift can keep you from developing the flexibility you need to be successful.

Growing up, I wanted to be an actress. Starting in elementary school, I performed in plays and musicals, took voice lessons, and even muddled my way through some dance classes. I was convinced that I was going to end up a Broadway star. I believed in my dream so much that I was willing to skip birthday parties and family vacations to go to rehearsals. I even remember one moment, in middle school, being down on my knees in my bedroom, crying to the heavens, "If I can just please get this part, I don't care if I NEVER have a boyfriend!" That's a pretty valuable bargain coming from a seventh-grade girl who wouldn't have minded some attention from the boys.

My dream started to come true in my senior year of high school. While I was starring in one of the school plays, an envelope arrived. I had been accepted into the competitive New York University musical theatre program. I moved to New York City and took four years of classes with some of the best teachers in the country, preparing to be a stage actress.

And then…

My senior year of college, something changed. It happened slowly. My friends and I had started auditioning for shows, both in New York and regionally. Some of my friends handled the rejection with grace and poise. They were pragmatic about every "no." They didn't take it personally when they made it all the way through three callbacks but ultimately didn't get cast in a role. I, however, felt every rejection acutely. I hated the underlying feeling that there were always 100 other actresses right outside the door who could sing higher than me, kick higher than me, look prettier than me. I hated feeling replaceable.

That spring, I was walking along 14th Street, thinking about how real life as an actor involved more time trying to *get* a role than it did actually *performing* in a role. I was mentally wrestling with whether I could come to grips with my dislike of rejection and get excited about auditions. As I turned to walk along the park at Union Square, the following thought popped into my mind:

*I don't want to be famous. I want to be **important**. And that's different.*

When I was a child, being famous and being important felt like the same thing. We look up to athletes, actors, entrepreneurs, and politicians. We admire the people we see on TV and read about in magazines. I thought that being famous would make me important. But I realized—it doesn't have to be that way.

As the thought crystallized in my mind, I took it further:

I want to have a job where people are HAPPY I show up to work every day. Not a job where I feel replaceable, like acting. Remember, I even had that director who called actors "warm props," like we were nothing more than walking, talking set decorations! I hate feeling replaceable. I need to be somewhere where people care that I showed up that day. I don't care if no one gives me a standing ovation when I leave work in the evening; that's not the point. I just need to be needed. I need to be important.

In that moment when I realized that being famous and being important aren't the same thing, my entire career plan shifted. I was weeks away from graduating with one of the most coveted acting degrees in the world, but I just couldn't be an actress anymore. Acting had been my plan, but the life of an actor wasn't what I wanted. If what I really wanted in life was to feel like my contributions were important, being an actress wasn't the only—or even the best—way to accomplish that. I needed to change my life plan to enable me to reach my real goal. So I did.

It's a common story: we set our goals based on our desires at a certain point in our life. And society tells us that we shouldn't give up on our dreams or else we're quitters. But most of us reach a point in life when our plans don't seem to be working for us. So we have to choose either to change our plans or to fight for something that doesn't serve us.

At some point in our lives,
we'll likely have to choose between
changing our plans or fighting for
something that doesn't serve us.

The Science of Letting Go

I wanted to understand how people deal with adapting when their plans aren't working out, so I commissioned a study on the topic. My research team and I interviewed over 1,000 people about their ability to navigate change and their feelings about having to switch up their game plans when faced with a challenge. We asked the participants whether they feel like they can "learn as they go" in life when a project or situation is unfamiliar. Only 26 percent of respondents indicated having a strong belief that they could take in new information and learn while in the middle of a challenge. That means almost three-fourths of respondents DIDN'T feel like they could learn as they go and instead preferred to fall back into old patterns and habits.[1]

Those old patterns and habits are like a story. A story we've told ourselves over time and repeated again and again until we become convinced that it culminates in a happy ending. We cling to the story we've written for our lives and won't let go. This "life plan" is part of the reason why people reject change.

Resilient people can let go of a story that no longer serves them—a story that no longer makes sense. To be truly resilient in the face of change and challenges, we have to be less committed to a specific version of life and instead be willing to rewrite the story.

But we can't even start to rewrite our new story without first throwing away the old story. The old story tends to creep back in and cloud our thinking. It can happen to individuals but also to organizations.

Getting Unstuck from Old Ways

Back in 1991, researchers at Texas A&M University conducted a study with engineering students. They split the students into two groups, Group A and Group B. Both groups were given the same challenge: design the best bike rack possible. Group A first received a lengthy presentation on the design flaws within the current bike rack models. They learned why current designs were considered unwieldy and hard to get the bikes into. They learned about problems with the materials and production process. Group B received no information about the current bike rack models. They simply were told to design the best bike rack possible, and then they were dismissed.

At the end of several weeks, the two groups reconvened to present their designs. Group A presented first, and their team had come up with several improvements over the current bike rack model. Overall, the improvements were modest. They were small tweaks on the problematic design flaws.

Group B, having received no detailed instructions about the design challenges of past bike racks, presented second. When Group B showed off their designs, the study leaders were surprised to see that Group B had come up with vast improvements over current bike rack designs—modifications far superior to the ideas presented by Group A. Additionally, Group B had completed sketches for several alternative options, all of which were unique and creative improvements on the existing bike rack design.

Study leaders realized that without the mental constraints of seeing how the problem had been solved before, Group B engineers were free to think up unusual and effective solutions. Group A, on the other hand, had been subtly influenced by learning about the traditional bike rack solutions. The researchers called this phenomenon "design fixation."[2] Our brains can get fixated on "the way it's always been done" and struggle to move forward.

Design fixation in individuals isn't much different. We get seduced by comfortable beliefs and familiar strategies. Our brains even perceive things that are familiar as being a safer and smarter bet than an unknown path (it's called familiarity bias), even if what is familiar to us is actually holding us back. In order to combat design fixation in our lives, we have to begin to see the value in branching out and exploring new possibilities.

In my research, some of the study participants had a high level of something called "tolerance for ambiguity." These individuals reported being comfortable in new situations, where the outcome wasn't always clear. And that comfort level translated directly to success: those individuals with a high tolerance for ambiguity were in fact better at handling themselves during a challenge.

If you struggle with feeling frustrated in ambiguous situations with no obvious "right answer" or where you don't know what to do next, you aren't alone. It's a skill we don't spend much time developing, because it's easier to live in a world with clear-cut choices and paths to follow. People who have faced challenging situations before and come out on top tend to have an easier time navigating tricky situations in the future. Age can also play a role: study respondents ages 36 to 45 years old said they're willing to tolerate ambiguous situations confidently, which was the highest out of any age group.

Increasing your tolerance for ambiguity is possible. Below are two strategies for doing so.

Strategy 1: Recall What Worked in the Past

First, think about past experiences when you were heading into an unknown situation. If you struggle to start your list, remember that as children we faced unknown situations with much greater frequency than we do in adulthood. Kids walk into a new classroom with a new teacher every single year! They try new sports and activities regularly. They make new friends or say goodbye when old friends move away. Teenagers pack up all their belongings and go off to college. They go to their first dance, or on their first date. Young adults start their first job and pay their first bill. Every time you do something for the first time, you're heading into the unknown and facing ambiguity. In fact, children may be better at letting go of the plan than adults are, maybe because they do it more often! (More on that later in this chapter.)

Being able to point to a list of times you successfully navigated an ambiguous situation is a good first step. Next, think about what actions you took in those situations that helped you get through them. Did you keep an open mind? Did you control your anxiety? Did you befriend and lean on someone else going through the experience? Remembering the strategies that worked for you in the past is a good tactic, because each person is unique.

Remind yourself that each of those ambiguous situations was ultimately resolved. It was unknown and uncomfortable in the beginning, yet at some point your path became clear. Whether the end was enjoyable or successful (and I hope many of them were!), the situation didn't stay a mystery forever.

Strategy 2: Differentiate Between Plans and Goals

Another way to get more comfortable with ambiguity is to realize that letting go of the plan isn't the same as letting go of your goals. Being forced to change your plans doesn't lessen your chances of success. It may change your methods of success or your timeline. Or it may change the *type* of success you achieve. That's what happened for me.

Being forced to change your plans doesn't lessen your chances of success; it simply changes your methods of success.

When I left the world of performing arts, I thought it was for good. I put my creativity and communication skills into action in another way—working in public relations for corporations and nonprofit organizations. I gave TV interviews and built community engagement and marketing plans. But one day someone said to me, "I love the passion you have when you talk. You'd be a great motivational speaker." That moment shifted everything for me.

Now I'm back to using the performing skills I developed at NYU, but in a completely different way than I ever expected. This isn't the version of success I dreamed about when I was 12, but it's still success. In fact, I could argue that it's even *better* success, because I'm able to run my own business and create my own opportunities in a way that I'm not sure I would have been able to do in a traditional acting career.

There's always more than one route to your goals. You just have to be willing to find the best path for you.

Practicing for Change

If we hope to ever throw out the old plan and find a new one, one of the first hurdles we have to overcome is the discomfort of change. Change is usually accompanied by feelings of uncertainty, fear, and even sadness, all emotions we'd like to avoid if we could. But if we avoid those emotions and therefore avoid change, we're also avoiding growth.

Think about it like this: When it comes to our physical bodies, we're taught "no pain, no gain." If you want to be successful at a sport, for example, you know you have to push through the tough moments—the long workouts, the injuries—to get to the victory at the end. With enough practice and enough physical challenge (and the discomfort that comes with it), we can transform ourselves into people who are ready to compete.

So when it comes to our emotional lives, why do we avoid practicing for change? Why do we try to sidestep the discomfort that change brings instead of regularly practicing managing it in small ways so that we're prepared when a big change hits?

Here's one reason I think most of us have a problem: we think dealing with change requires change to happen first, and then we respond afterward. We're reactive when it comes to change instead of proactive. We let change tell US where it's going, and then we have to play catch-up to succeed.

Well, how can I tell change where to go? you're likely wondering. *I can't predict every change before it happens.*

That's true. You can't predict every change before it happens. But you can, with reasonable certainty, predict that change *is* going to happen. It always does. So, you can be nimble and flexible, prepared for circumstances to shift in response to an ever-changing world.

Lilian had worked at a mid-sized company for eight years. She liked her colleagues and many elements of her job, but as the company grew she was getting frustrated with the introduction of new processes, technology, and systems to help streamline information. It seemed like there was always some new initiative being introduced that was supposed to make their work easier and better, but really it just felt like there was more to learn on top of her already full list of tasks.

Lilian felt pulled in too many directions. She went to her manager and asked for help prioritizing her different projects and learning the new technology. She was hoping her manager would say, "You're right, Lilian. You have too much on your plate to waste time becoming proficient in this system. Why don't you just skip it and go back to managing your projects the way you used to?" Instead, Lilian's manager was frustrated, too. She reminded Lilian again that the software, once Lilian learns it, will actually save Lilian time. In addition, having all the information centralized in one place will help the entire team communicate. Lilian's manager ended the meeting by confirming that Lilian will have to adopt the new system by the end of the month.

Sometimes we want things to change, yet WE don't want to change. We passively wish we could change our circumstances while still staying within our comfort zone. But situations can't change if people don't change. To make change less frustrating and more tolerable, we need to be on the leading end of change. Instead of waiting for change to move us, we need to be ready to direct change in a way that works for us.

You can't predict every change
before it happens. But you can,
with reasonable certainty, predict that
change is going to happen.

Some people are better at this kind of flexibility than others, depending on factors like age and how long they've been in their career. In the study I conducted, younger employees had the easiest time being flexible about abandoning the status quo and "the way we've always done it" compared to employees who had been in their jobs longer. That could be because the younger employees hadn't had as much time to embrace the routines of the past, nor were they as likely to see those routines as having played a role in their success.

Overall, self-reported adaptability skills were lowest for older employees, with participants in this age range reporting not feeling as excited for new challenges. Because this age group values predictability and routine in their work, they were the least enthusiastic about new ways of working. American author Pearl S. Buck was known for saying, "You can judge your age by the amount of pain you feel when you come in contact with a new idea." The routines of age can leave us less flexible and less open to new ways of being, which adds to the pain of change.

When the Ground Shifts

Whatever your age or however many times you've faced change, it's easy to feel knocked off course when life doesn't go the way you expect.

That's how it felt when I was 26.

I had finally found my new path after leaving the acting world. I was working in the nonprofit sector, helping organizations communicate their mission to the community and raise money for good causes. I was a newlywed, a new homeowner, and a new dog mom living in a new city. I was starting over fresh, and the path was clear in front of me.

Until it wasn't.

Part of moving to a new town is finding all new doctors. My new dermatologist had taken a few biopsies of my skin, but she wasn't worried. "You have very fair skin," she said, "but none of these moles look suspicious. And because you stay out of the sun, that's a good thing. We'll check out these two spots because you're new here, but I'm sure they're normal." I'd had biopsies before that turned out to be nothing (the curse of pale skin!), so I put it out of my mind for almost a month.

I took a weekend trip to a spa to celebrate getting settled into my new "adult" life. A spa vacation sounded like a very grown-up thing to do. Since I was feeling so responsible, I decided to get into the peaceful vacation vibe and turn off my cell phone for the weekend so I could really relax. I got a massage and a salt scrub, went to daily yoga classes, took a hike up a small mountain nearby, and read straight through two e-books in three days (the only tech device I turned on the whole time).

During the drive home Sunday night, I forgot my cell phone was still turned off. As I pulled onto my street, I reached into my bag and hit the power button. I walked into the living room and noticed a voicemail message alert on my home screen. It had come in earlier that night. Hitting play, I walked over to the sofa, but before I could sit down I heard my doctor's voice:

"Courtney, the biopsy came back. It's melanoma. That's the bad kind of skin cancer. It looks deep—deeper than the biopsy we took. You're going to need surgery to get the rest of the tumor. Please call my office in the morning so we can figure out a plan."

The next several days were a blur of doctor's appointments, second and third opinions, wrangling with insurance, and booking surgery. I'd had practice making difficult decisions before, but this was the first time in my life I was making decisions where my life literally

32

hung in the balance. During those days, I clung to every decision I could make, like which surgeon to choose, where to have surgery, and when to operate. I couldn't control my cancer, but having power over those small choices was my saving grace. It made me feel like I wasn't completely helpless.

Recovering from surgery was tough. While the surgery itself was minor, I had a bad reaction to the anesthesia that left me vomiting on the floor of the cancer hospital. My newlywed husband, also stressed from the abrupt shift our life had taken in the last several weeks, seemed grossed out by my being sick.

"Get back in the bed," he hollered, while I rested my cheek on the coolness of the hospital floor. "That's disgusting. You're embarrassing me."

His words made me want to barf even more.

Even as I struggled to keep from throwing up again, a small part of me realized in the split second he spoke that my health wasn't the only thing that was changing. My entire life needed to change. Including my marriage.

The process of letting go wasn't easy. To let go, I had to first work through my grief over what I thought was "supposed" to happen.

We don't always think of it this way, but change almost always brings some level of grieving. Grieving for what we expected to happen. Grieving for what we worked so hard to accomplish. Grieving for what we thought we had earned or deserved. Grieving for a vision of the future that will never come true—because although our goal might not change, it's often the case that our path to it must, and success feels and looks different in this altered course.

If you ignore grief as part of changing your plans, you may never be successful at making change happen. A part of you may always be wondering, *What if all this had never happened? Would that old version of my life have been better?* It's a little like those high school athletes who still spend every weekend hanging out at the bar with their decades-old clique of friends, regaling strangers with the story of their state championship win: They can't move on because they're stuck in the past. They are unable to envision their life beyond the locker room.

By admitting that you might have some grief around a plan that didn't turn out the way you expected, you're not giving up. You're actually starting the process of moving on. When you admit your grief, you can address it. And when you address your grief, you can put it behind you in a healthy way.

Choosing Change

Wouldn't it be easier if only one thing changed at a time? Maybe, but it often doesn't work that way. Sometimes, when we're forced against our will to alter our course, that shift causes a crack in the foundation somewhere else. It's up to us to decide between ignoring the cracks and risking them getting bigger or addressing the cracks by choosing even more change.

We can disregard the changes happening around us, wasting our time in denial that change is inevitable. Or we can take hold of the reins and turn unwanted change into change that's ultimately positive.

We can waste our time in denial that change is inevitable. Or we can take hold of the reins and turn unwanted change into change that's ultimately positive.

Several months later, when I was back on my feet, I filed for divorce. I never pictured myself divorced before my 27th birthday. It went against everything I had planned and expected for my life. But being unhappy went against my plans, too. Either way, I was going to sacrifice something I wanted. I had to choose which loss I was willing to live with and which cost was too high.

When you cling so tightly to your plans, you run the risk of missing out on something even better than you could have ever expected. You can't write a new plan if you don't let go of your old plans. It's time to stop fighting the change that's coming and get ready to let go.

Chapter 2

What's Your Gut Got to Do with It?

"It is not a failure to readjust my sails to fit the
waters I find myself in."—Mackenzi Lee

*W*hat keeps us wanting to stick to the plan, even when we know we need to let it go? Who—or what—is to blame for our unwillingness to change?

Two words: your gut.

It's common guidance when making decisions to "go with your gut." We've been led to believe that our "gut" is a helpful instinct that automatically knows the correct answer. If we rely on our "gut," we're promised that our internal compass will automatically lead us to the right choices.

In your life, you've been presented with a tough decision. Maybe as a child you had to decide whether to go to summer camp or to play on a traveling sports team that conflicted with the camp schedule. "Well, what does your gut say you should do?" your parents may have asked. Or you interviewed for several jobs and got an offer for one, but it's not your top choice. Now you're left to decide whether to accept the offer or hold out and see if you get an offer for the other job. And if you do get an offer for the other job, can you be *sure* that job would be better? "Do a gut check," your friend suggests.

So does your gut always have the right answer? No, not exactly.

Sometimes your gut can steer you wrong. Here's an example of how that happens: What color is a frog? If "green" immediately popped into your brain, you're right. But…you're not completely right. Frogs come in every color of the rainbow, including red, yellow, and blue. Some frogs can even change colors! Green is just the color of the frog we see most often in our daily lives or illustrated in pictures, so it's what comes to mind first. It's our "gut" response.

Let's try again.

I'm thinking of a numerical pattern. It starts like this: 1, 2, _____. What's the missing number in the series? If you thought of 3, you're sort of right again. Three isn't a wrong answer. But the answer could easily be 4, because $1 + 1 = 2$, and $2 + 2 = 4$. Most people answer 3 because 1, 2, 3 is the most common way we see that series of numbers.

When one choice is well-known and the other choice is unfamiliar, like in the examples above, it's especially likely that your gut will steer you wrong. That's because the phenomenon of "gut instinct" is actually a biological phenomenon. Part of your nervous system is located in your intestines, and those nerves in your gut DO send signals to your brain. Sometimes those signals are saying, "This is new and unusual! I don't feel comfortable!" So your gut instinct recognizes one choice as more secure, because the old choice doesn't fire off the same warning alerts as the unfamiliar choice does.

Going with your gut leads to the most common answer. Your gut knows the status quo. It gives you "the way you've always done it." And that's perfectly okay…if you're solving a problem you've solved hundreds of times before. If you're working on a situation that you've dealt with daily for years, then going with your gut is the simplest, best way to take action on a problem. Your gut instinct will be correct because your gut has been down this path before.

But if you're in a situation you've never been in before, your gut doesn't know what's right and what's wrong. If you're solving a problem you've never solved before, like facing a health scare or a global pandemic or your first corporate merger, your gut is in new territory. It can't help you. If you listen only to your gut, you'll never be able to accomplish anything new or noteworthy.

To be successful at letting go of the plan, you have to learn to override your gut instinct and feel comfortable in new territory.

Learn to override your gut instinct and feel comfortable in new territory.

Are You Running on Autopilot?

There was a time in your life when you were probably more comfortable with new territory than you are now. Children consistently have a higher acceptance of fluidity than adults. Not all kids, of course, but many. Think about how days are designed for school-children: they move from one class to another, one room to another, one teacher to another, all day long. The month of October and the month of July are entirely different experiences for kids, thanks to the typical school calendar. Every year, kids encounter different teachers and different classmates. Many adults can't even stand it if you swap out their desk chair or add an unexpected meeting to their calendar!

Can you imagine if your boss was sick and sent a "substitute boss" to manage you for the day? The kind of low-level daily upheaval that's considered "normal" for kids would be unbearable for many adults.

Then, around age 18, everything changes again. It's time to either pack up your life and move away to college, without any of your family, or end your schooling and start your career. You move in with roommates or live alone for the first time, responsible for yourself.

Anna and Mateo were nervous about how their kids would deal with change. When they thought about the job offer, they were torn. It would be such a step up for Mateo's career and lots more money, but it meant a big move across the country. They'd be leaving behind family, their support network, and all their sons' friends. Hugo and Samuel were nine and seven, and they'd been at the same school since pre-K, so they'd known their friends for years. School days were spent carpooling the neighborhood kids from school to soccer games, and summer days were spent with both boys riding bikes around the neighborhood with all their friends.

Anna didn't want Hugo and Sam to have to start over in a new school with new teachers. Mateo worried that the boys would have a hard time making new friends, especially Hugo, since he'd be coming in during fifth grade, the last year of elementary school, when friendships were already set. The move would mean Sam would miss playing on his favorite T-ball team. There were so many things that the family would be leaving behind.

Ultimately, Anna and Mateo decided to take the risk and make the move. They sat the boys down and broke the news to them.

"Will I have a new bedroom?" Sam asked. Anna confirmed he would. "Can I paint it whatever color I want? Ooh! Can I get those sticky stars and put them on the ceiling of my new room?"

"Of course you can."

Sam seemed happy. Excited, even.

Hugo was quiet. After a few moments, he spoke up. "Will I be able to come back? Will I be able to visit Noah and Ben and Connor?"

"Yes, sweetheart. We're going to come back and visit a lot, because Nonna and Papi live here."

Hugo left to tell his friends the news.

By the time moving day came around, the boys were little bundles of energy. On the way to the airport, both boys handed out stickers to their friends with their new address, phone number, and Anna's email address on them. Sam whispered to Connor, "My mom said I can get a phone when I start middle school. Then we can TEXT!"

"Cool!" Connor whispered back.

The boys slept on the plane and during most of the drive to their new home. As they pulled into the driveway, the boys tumbled out of the car to see their new bedrooms. "Woah, look how big the backyard is!" "Mom, can we get soccer nets?" "This one is my room!" The excitement over their new environment continued until they finally crashed early at 8:30 P.M.

In bed that night, Anna and Mateo marveled at how positive the boys had been.

"Did you notice how they always found something positive to focus on?" Anna remarked. "They're excited about new bedrooms, the backyard. Sam is thrilled that moving cross-country means he's going to get a cell phone. They're just finding all the GOOD things

41

about this move, instead of being scared. Maybe this will go better than we thought."

When people talk about children being resilient, it's not surprising. Kids are little change warriors, dealing with small changes nearly every day, yet they have no real power to control their surroundings. They EXPECT change to happen and be out of their control, so most of them are used to it. They've made CHANGE the habit, instead of stasis. They don't live on autopilot.

As adults, we go through a lot of life on autopilot. Autopilot is what happens when you're driving to work but don't really remember getting there because the routine has become such a habit that you tune out the details. You don't have to pay close attention to the directions because you just *know* that there's a left turn here, a stop sign up ahead, and you better slow down because you're coming up to a school zone.

Autopilot gets a bad rap, but it isn't all bad. Autopilot can help you conserve the energy of your thought processes to allow you to focus on more important things. Once you get good at tying your shoes, for example, you don't have to focus so hard. You can simultaneously tie your shoes and hold a conversation.

But autopilot can work against you in other ways. It can make it easy to slip back into old habits without thinking about it. Autopilot is easy, and easy is tempting, especially when so much of life feels hard. Why NOT take a little shortcut here or there when you can? I'm all for simplifying when it's appropriate. But slipping back into old patterns and habits that aren't serving you anymore only *feels* easy. In the long run, you're making your life harder, because you're prolonging the inevitable change that's coming down the horizon—without preparing for it.

Strategy 1: Focus on What's NOT Changing

When everything is changing, it feels like it might be easier to cling to as much familiarity as possible. But we often cling to the wrong things: old habits, old beliefs, old processes. Change will get easier if you remind yourself that not *everything* is changing. I promise, that almost never happens! Something is staying consistent: your family, your hobbies, your friends, your skills and talents. And THOSE factors are more important than habits. So yes, you may have to let go of some things. And that feels uncomfortable. But some important parts—parts that make your life enjoyable and make you YOU—are remaining.

When things feel like they're changing all around you, it's important to remember what's staying the same. The more you can mentally return to the consistent elements of your life and remind yourself of what ISN'T changing, the less frustrating change will feel.

Strategy 2: Adopt "Beginner's Mind"

Another strategy to try is something called "beginner's mind." Beginner's mind is the concept of approaching a task you've already mastered with a fresh perspective. Try to wipe your mind clean of expectations and what you "know" to be true. The point of beginner's mind is to get rid of the preconceived notions you might have about how an experience is supposed to turn out.

When it comes to dealing with change, having the mind of a beginner can make you more open to letting go of your original plan and being flexible. With beginner's mind, you can more easily move from expectation mode to edit mode.

Reexamining Your Mental Script

The week after my college graduation, I started my first job in New York City. The very definition of being a beginner! I got hired at a marketing company called GoCard. Brands would hire us to create postcards that were usually displayed on a rack in bars and restaurants in major cities. The postcards were funny, sexy, edgy advertisements—the kind of thing you might take home and put up on the wall of your first apartment.

The higher-ups gave me the sales training. I read the sales manual. After weeks of preparation, my boss finally handed me my list, and I started to make calls.

It was slow going at first. I was new and awkward at trying to get prospective clients to agree to a meeting. Around call 28, I started getting into my groove. At call 52, I booked an appointment. It was time to prepare for my first sales meeting. I studied my sales manual until I knew every line. I had every word of the sales script memorized. I knew how to describe the production methods, the turnaround time. I could explain the locations the prospect's cards would be in. I could justify the costs. Any objection they might have, I knew how to counter it.

And then I walked in.

I met with two people, Greg and Regina. I presented all my material, described all the features and benefits in great detail. And with every line from the sales script, I watched Greg and Regina pay less and less attention.

What was I doing wrong? I knew I was saying the script right! What could I have forgotten?

And then Regina said the words that changed my entire career:

"What do companies even PUT on these cards?"

In that moment, it hit me: I was talking about features and benefits, but the client couldn't even envision what a card advertising her company would look like. I was 12 steps down the road, and I'd left her back at the starting line. The sales script had been missing a big chunk of important, basic information, and nobody had noticed it until now.

I closed the mental script in my head. I picked up a pencil and my notepad and started to draw (poorly). I sketched out a three-frame cartoon explaining Greg and Regina's brand in a fun, visually interesting way. And by the end of our meeting, Greg and Regina had ordered a small run of postcards with my concept on them. My first sale!

Having a mental script can be helpful. That script I got at my first job wasn't WRONG. It just wasn't...complete. I didn't know enough yet about how to read the room, and that lesson wasn't in the guidebook. We think of experts as always having the right answers, but sometimes beginners catch things that experts miss. My colleagues who had been there a long time took the script for granted. They assumed it was just fine because it worked for them. But they had instincts honed from years of practice. Without that background, the script was incomplete. It took me, coming in with my fresh perspective, to point out the gap.

Some scripts you'll get are incomplete, like mine was. Some scripts are out of date. Some scripts aren't even scripts at all, just messages you've gotten from other people telling you this is the way you're SUPPOSED to do it.

When you examine your expectations for your life, who wrote that script? Was it you? Was it your parents? Your teachers? Oftentimes, we hear voices in our heads telling us a story of what we should be, what we can't be, what our skills are, or what our value is. If you're holding on to a script in your head that you didn't write, that's a sure sign that the script needs to be thrown out.

If you're holding on to a script you didn't write, throw it out—it's time to write a new one with YOUR voice.

Who benefits from the script? Your boss? Your kids? Your partner? Yourself? Frequently, our mental scripts serve everyone else—but at the expense of ourselves. I'm a big believer in giving back to other people, but as someone once told me, "You can't pour from an empty cup." That phrase is now near and dear to my heart, because I realized I can't give more than I have. And if someone wrote your script for you AND they are benefiting from the script? That's a warning sign to examine how much control that person has over your life.

To start examining your mental script, write down ten thoughts you tell yourself on a regular basis. Most people's lists include items like "I should lose weight." "If I'd gotten that other degree, I'd be making more money." "I have trouble dating because I'm too picky." "Family always comes first." "I'm good at math."

Why do you hold those beliefs? Who first planted the seed that grew into those ideas about your life, career, intellect, abilities, or looks? Often, so much time has passed between the seed being planted and today that we don't even realize we've taken someone else's thought and made it part of our own belief system—we've taken other people's expectations and turned them into our own script.

And even if you DID write the script for your life, that doesn't mean you should keep it. Your script might be outdated, just like the one at my first job. You may think that by keeping it, you're being optimistic that you can still "make it come true." Or you might believe, deep inside, that if you sacrifice the script and all your expectations, you'll be giving up—failing.

Your Gut Versus Grit

When it comes to being resilient, tenacity and grit are seen as positive traits. But if they're overused, tenacity and grit can be harmful. Caroline Adams Miller, the author of *Getting Grit*, calls this "stupid grit"—clinging to something that isn't meant for you.

How do we know the right situations to apply tenacity and grit? How do we know when to keep going? And how do we know when we're pushing toward the wrong goal and it would be smarter to give up and try something else?

Think about it like this: If every time you eat ice cream you get sick 20 minutes later, you probably would decide to stop eating ice cream. Stupid grit would be to keep eating ice cream just because it tastes good. But you don't stop eating food altogether simply because ice cream makes you sick! That would be giving up completely. You don't even have to stop eating dessert—you just have to stop eating ice cream.

Smart grit, as defined by Miller, is figuring out what's not working for you and removing it. Then you're free to make a revision and replace what's not working with something new!

There's a big grocery store chain here in Texas that Texans are REALLY proud of called H-E-B. H-E-B is a bit of a local treasure in Texas, because of their great selection and high-quality in-house brand. And H-E-B is also a proud donor to many nonprofit organizations in the community. So they have a well-earned reputation for excellence.

H-E-B was ready for the coronavirus. They have an entire full-time emergency response team who had been paying attention to what was happening in China. The emergency response team members were talking with grocery store counterparts in Asia, trying to prepare. As soon as COVID-19 cases hit Texas, H-E-B started using food service companies that had been providing hot food for school lunches but weren't anymore, since schools were closed, to reallocate that food that would have been wasted to H-E-B stores. So not only did they preserve their supply chain, but they also helped keep smaller food provider affiliates in business by purchasing from them instead of canceling orders.

But for all the good things H-E-B did on a large scale to be ready, it's what they did on an individual scale that was the most impressive. One of their employees, Alma, worked for H-E-B corporate head-quarters as a bookkeeper. She'd been a bookkeeper in the corporate office for years and hadn't been on an actual retail floor in a long time—until the epidemic, when toilet paper and canned beans started becoming the must-have items for 2020. People flooded into grocery stores across America, and Alma raised her hand. Alma said, "I've never worked a cash register, but if someone will teach me, I'd love to help." Alma stepped right onto the front lines, face to face with hundreds of humans an hour, giving them a smile and making sure they got what they needed.

How often have you heard things like this at work:

- "That's not *our* division's problem."

- "That's not the way we've always done it."

- "Things need to change around here. Oh, but I don't mean me. *I* don't need to change…"

That's not how Alma acted. She saw a need, and she volunteered to fill it. She would have been well within her rights to say, "Well, that's not my problem to fix. I'm just an accountant," or "What can *I* do to help? I work in the corporate office." But thankfully for those of us who needed toilet paper, she didn't. Instead of doing the work she always does, Alma took a risk and stepped up to fill a much-needed role.

Sometimes disregarding your gut instinct means rethinking everything you did to achieve your current level of success. Most of us got to where we are by figuring out what works. And if something stops working, we try to fix it. We tweak it, and we problem-solve, and we attempt to put it back in working order. But when the whole world is changing around us, fixes and solutions aren't enough. We have to stop trying "fixes" and "tweaks" to avoid having to change.

We have to stop trying "fixes" and "tweaks"
to avoid having to change.

When you "go with your gut," you're clinging to an idea that feels "right," probably because it's comfortable or safe or has worked in the past. But just because something feels right doesn't make it so. Going with your gut is often just providing a sense of false control over the situation at hand.

Instead, try to approach your fork in the road with beginner's mind. Recognize that you're making assumptions about the change or about your options, and try to wipe those assumptions out of your mind. You don't know everything that's coming, and it's okay not to know. It may not feel good, but it's part of navigating change and coming out on the other side. If you can face uncertainty with beginner's mind instead of your gut, you'll be less likely to feel frustrated and angry. And you'll be more likely to succeed—with a new script that will serve you much better because it has been updated or completely rewritten in your own voice.

Remember: Your gut hasn't been here before. Your gut doesn't know what to do. Don't let it butt in and tell you what to do next. Be the boss of your gut and guide it, instead of letting it guide you.

Meet the ReVisionary

Samuel Adams

Founding Father, Business Failure

Long before his face and name graced the front of beer bottles, Samuel Adams had a rocky career. He was fired from his first job after being distracted from his work by politics, so his wealthy father lent him money to start a new business. Adams quickly lost that money, so his father hired him at the family malthouse. When his father died and he inherited the business, Adams ran the once-successful business into bankruptcy within a few short years.

Without his father or his father's money to rescue him any longer, Adams changed paths. His fascination with politics had always been a distraction from focusing on business anyway, so he decided to follow his passion.

Adams became a primary organizer of the Sons of Liberty and worked to oppose British taxation in the colonies. He served as a spokesperson for the American Revolution and became well known for his passionate and knowledgeable speeches that stirred crowds to action. Adams was a signer of the Declaration of Independence, and Thomas Jefferson called him "truly the man of the Revolution."

Adams may have had a terrible head for business, but his failure allowed him to prosper in politics, where he truly belonged.

Chapter 3

The Hidden Benefit of Change

"We cannot become what we want to be by
remaining what we are."—Max de Pree

*W*hen Colleen Barrett couldn't afford law school, she decided to go to junior college to become a legal secretary. Shortly after graduation, she got hired to assist a rising lawyer in San Antonio, Texas, named Herb Kelleher. Colleen's work earned Herb's respect, and he began mentoring Colleen in his legal practice. As the years went on, Herb became a founder of Southwest Airlines, eventually taking over as chairman and then CEO. Colleen became an employee at Southwest, first serving as Herb's corporate secretary. But Herb never stopped recognizing Colleen's contributions, and over time she rose through the ranks.

First, Colleen became the vice president of administration at Southwest Airlines, and later the vice president of customers. As VP of customers, Colleen instituted the famous Southwest Airlines company culture. Southwest flight attendants, for example, are allowed to deliver the pre- and post-flight announcements with their own personal flair, leading to singing, dancing, and poetry welcoming customers onto their flight. These safety-briefing announcements aren't optional; they're required by law. But that doesn't mean they have to be done the same, boring way every time. Under Colleen's leadership, employees were allowed to add a little fun into their day— and their customers' day, too.

Colleen also spearheaded the policy of taking care of employees first and customers second, which was seen as a wild departure from the typical "the customer is always right" mindset. But Colleen's belief was that happy, cared-for employees would provide top-notch customer service, which would therefore mean customers would have an enjoyable experience. Annual customer satisfaction surveys seem to prove Colleen's point: Southwest customers prefer flying the airline over any other. Year after year, Southwest has been at the top of the industry in terms of passenger volume, profitability, customer satisfaction, and low employee turnover. By thinking differently about customer service with Colleen's help, Southwest Airlines found its place in the crowded travel industry.

Ultimately, Colleen Barrett took over as the president and chief operating officer of Southwest, making her not just the first woman president of the company, but also the first woman president of any airline. Over the course of her career, she went from a woman who couldn't afford to earn a legal degree to the leader of a profitable major company. Colleen's flexibility allowed her not only to adjust her own personal path, but also to see Southwest's road to success in a different light.

While there's nothing wrong with having a plan, Colleen's story shows how sometimes taking an unexpected path provides surprising benefits. If she hadn't been willing to revise her plan, she might never have ended up at the top of one of the most well-known brands in the United States. In this chapter, we'll take a look at how making revisions often serves you in ways you never would have anticipated. If you're able to reframe your expectations when the unexpected strikes and see success as a moving target, you're more likely to find success wherever it might be hiding—and you'll feel less stressed and develop more resilience along the way. When you do this, you'll discover that "lost plans" are never really lost if you can find and seize the opportunity within them.

"Lost plans" are never really lost
if you can find and seize the
opportunity within them.

The artist Anna Mary Robertson (1860–1961) is a great example of flexibility. She married and gave birth to ten children, which wasn't uncommon for a young woman of her era. Her mother raised her to be a homemaker, and she had little time for hobbies. Robertson took care of her family and spent her time sewing dresses, doing embroidery, and working around the house. After her children were grown, Robertson still prided herself on the homemaking skills her mother had taught her, even though she didn't enjoy them. But then her husband died. And then the arthritis set in. Robertson could no longer do the delicate needlework that used to occupy her time.

When that happened, Anna Mary Robertson made a major shift. She put aside the needlework that her arthritis wouldn't let her finish, and she picked up a paintbrush. Despite being untrained, she began to practice her painting day after day. At age 78, Robertson started painting idyllic farm scenes. Her work got noticed by a collector, and "Grandma Moses" the painter was born.

Anna Mary Robertson wasn't famous, but Grandma Moses was. She exhibited her paintings until her nineties and lived to paint until age 101. Can you imagine if she'd put down the embroidery needle and decided she was too old to pick up anything new? Thank goodness for all her fans that she found a new way to fulfill herself, even near the end of her life. Thank goodness for all of us that we can find new ways to move through the world, even when our bodies give out, or our careers falter, or our relationships shift.

Flip...Without Flipping Out

Think about your high school math class. For most of us, the experience of high school math is pretty similar—consistent curriculum, nearly identical methods of teaching. The typical high school math experience looks like this: your teacher lectures for 40 minutes about, say, the quadratic equation. She asks if there are any questions. Then she assigns pages 74–75, questions 1–28, for homework.

After school, you go home and open up your math book. You turn to page 74 and start to answer question 1. You were listening in class. You watched the teacher solve the problems. But sitting there in your bedroom or at your dining table, it feels different. The problems seem harder, and your teacher isn't there to help. You answer the questions the best you can, but you trudge into math class the next day knowing you didn't get most of your homework completed. Even worse, today is going to be another lecture that builds on yesterday's quadratic equation lesson, so now you're likely to be even more confused.

But what if class didn't have to be that way?

Two Colorado high school teachers asked themselves that question in the early 2000s. Jonathan Bergmann and Aaron Sams were just looking for a way to help kids who had missed school because of illness. The two teachers realized that the recent rise in technology meant they could record a video lesson of their material and send it home with students who had been absent. That solved one problem for these teachers—helping students catch up on missed classroom time.

But they didn't stop there. The two teachers realized that their use of recordings could offer an even more valuable tool to help *all* students learn better. Bergmann and Sams started recording advance videos of their lectures. They assigned the lectures as "pre-work" to the students. Bergmann and Sams flipped the usual model: Instead of receiving a lecture during class time and then working on assigned problems at home by themselves, the students' nightly homework was to watch the recorded video lectures and get a basic understanding of the material. The next day in class, the problems that would usually be assigned as "homework" could be completed together, with the teacher right there to answer questions. In this way, the students were able to learn collaboratively by doing the work with their teacher as their guide.

This approach, now called the "flipped classroom model," didn't come out of nowhere. The Socratic method of learning, for example, has always allowed for students to ask questions, test their theories, and dialogue with their teachers. But for most of us, classroom instruction has looked pretty similar for decades. My son's high school math classes were structured just like my high school math classes, and mine looked just like my father's.

Kim Fromberg, an elementary school teacher with a decade of experience, discovered the flipped classroom model by accident when she volunteered to be a pilot teacher for a new technology initiative to have iPads in every classroom. When she started to integrate the flipped classroom model, Fromberg realized she was changing more than just her delivery style. She was changing how learning happened.

"Learning isn't just about teaching," Fromberg says. "It shouldn't be about the teacher and 'their way.' But that's how many classrooms are structured. The teacher is teaching the material in the style that's most convenient for them."

Fromberg recognized that when you turn the model around and put the student at the center of the equation, you come to realize that the typical classroom style may not be the best delivery system. The traditional "plan" for learning might not be the optimal way of reaching the desired end goal—student mastery of the concepts and enhanced critical thinking capabilities. As Fromberg put it: "The teacher teaching the material isn't the most important part of the classroom equation. It's whether or not the learner *learns* the material. That's the goal. And flipped learning makes that happen." It's a subtle shift, but an important one.

Flipped learning is the epitome of questioning "the way we've always done it." The model took a structure that has been embedded in our daily lives for generations and turned it on its head, with great outcomes. But it's hard to notice how things could be different when you're so used to seeing them a certain way.

You don't have to completely upend your standard procedures in order to reap the benefits of change. Sometimes all it takes is revising one element of your plan to experience greater success. That's why it's worth stepping back from a situation that seems like a problem or challenge and reframing it as a potential opportunity to be realized—it just needs a different approach. In the process, you'll likely discover that the discomfort of change pales in comparison to the reduced stress and tension that comes with a new way of doing things.

One small media company in New York City had friction between the two main departments that had been going on for years. The typical project at this company went like this: The salespeople would close a deal. The media team would have to deliver on what the salespeople had promised. Client expectations were often unrealistic because the media team was never consulted about the promises made by the salespeople. Nearly every day, clients would call their sales contact looking for status updates. And nearly every day, the sales team would turn to the media team and demand immediate information.

Often these conversations devolved into arguments. During one of these high-emotion arguments, a meeting was called to try to get everyone on the same page. Twenty minutes into the meeting-turned-fight, a newer employee on the media team raised her hand and posed the following question to the sales team: "If you're mad at US because your clients are mad at YOU, what if we could just keep the clients from getting mad at you in the first place? It seems like the clients just want more information, instead of feeling like they don't know what's going on. They feel out of the loop, so then when they get frustrated enough at the lack of information, they call you up and ask for an update. But they're already upset when they ask."

"What if we promised them a set schedule of updates?" she suggested. "What if they knew they'd hear from the media team every Tuesday and Friday with a report? That would do two things: first, it would help them feel informed, and it would also provide a way for the media team to talk directly to the client, which we haven't had before. That way we can talk to them about whether or not their expectations are realistic, and if they're not, maybe temper them before they get too far down the road."

Beginning that day, the entire company revised their processes: instead of waiting until clients asked for updates, updates were delivered twice a week unprompted. And the organization removed a source of friction that had become both external to their clients and internal to their employee relationships.

Where in your life are you just accepting the way things have always been? Where in your organization could you start to question if there's room for improvement? Healthy organizations and individuals don't make change just for the sake of making change. But they're always on the lookout for opportunities for change, where even slight shifts could make for a better situation.

Unexpected ≠ Unwanted

Sometimes a changed plan can be even better than you could have hoped. Think about all the experiences in your life you would have missed if the very first goal you made had to be set in stone. If we had to commit to our plans and never change, we'd all have careers as astronauts, veterinarians, and fairy princesses! Or you'd be married to the first person you had a crush on and stuck in the first low-paying position you thought was your dream job.

When you plan something, you have expectations. You decide what you want and you create a roadmap to achieve it. So when something unexpected comes along and derails that plan, it's natural to interpret that obstacle as "bad" or "a setback." But sometimes those unexpected obstacles turn out to have surprising payoffs.

To find the hidden benefit in revising your plans, start by looking for outcomes in your life that took you by surprise. For me, that was becoming a parent. I had PLANNED to be a parent, but then those plans were ripped away from me. Melanoma, the kind of cancer I had, means it's not a good idea to get pregnant for at least five years following diagnosis. If you do, you risk the cancer coming back. After five years, my doctor told me, I could get pregnant without fear. But then I was diagnosed with melanoma *again*, just a few years later. And then *again*, a few years after that.

During that time, I started working for a nonprofit organization called Planet Cancer that supports young adults with cancer. Through my work, I got messages from all over the country and the world from other young people fighting melanoma. Amy was the first one to message me. She was excited to see a fellow melanoma survivor working on staff at this organization. Amy had been diagnosed with melanoma in her twenties, just like me. She waited the five years to try to get pregnant, and she had been successful. But when her daughter was just three months old, Amy's cancer came roaring back. This time it was even more aggressive, and her doctor suggested the hormones of pregnancy and postpartum may have contributed to the fast-growing tumor he had removed from her back. Sadly, Amy didn't survive to be at her daughter's first birthday party.

After several of those stories, I decided getting pregnant was too risky for me. I was young, I told myself, and I had plenty of time to figure out what my life was going to look like. I could always adopt, friends told me. I could foster or volunteer with children. Or I could be the "cool aunt" that every kid loves. I tried to put it out of my mind. I threw all my maternal energy into starting up a local nonprofit in my hometown of Austin, Texas. The purpose of my nonprofit was to help other young people find a cause they cared about. I cared about animals, cancer, and kids aging out of the foster care system, so that's where I dedicated my time, money, and energy. Many young 20- and 30-somethings I met felt a pull to give back but hadn't yet discovered their nonprofit passion.

The model we created was simple: every month our young adult members contributed money automatically into the pot—just a small amount that wouldn't break the bank if they weren't used to regular donations. It would auto-debit right out of their account, so they wouldn't have to think about it, and it was just the price of a few cups of fancy coffee. Every member who donated that month then got a vote on where the money would go. Each month we had a different focus. For example, one month the focus would be homelessness, and they had to vote for one of three different nonprofits whose mission was to end homelessness. The winning nonprofit would receive the entire pot of everyone's donations, as well as three hours of our time on a service project. The next month, the focus might be literacy, and then animal welfare, and so on. The goal was that after being a part of this community of young adult volunteer-donors for one or two years, each member would find a nonprofit they loved and give to them directly.

One month the group voted to support a nonprofit whose mission was equal opportunity music lessons to kids whose parents couldn't afford it. The kids picked an instrument of their choice and got free music lessons, and they got to be a part of their school band AND the nonprofit's band. Just like I did every month, I asked the executive director of the nonprofit, "If you win the vote, how will you use our money and time? I bet you'll use our money to help pay for the music teachers. But how can you use our time? We can't teach music lessons."

Dylan, the executive director, responded, "You know what would be the most meaningful? If you could come talk to these kids about college. Not try to talk them INTO college, but just demystify the college experience: what it's like to apply, to have a roommate, to take a class only once a week, that kind of thing. Most of these kids are interested in college, but they don't even know a single person who has been to college."

So we threw a pizza party for these kids to give them an opportunity to talk casually with the young adult volunteers about the college experience. I gathered a couple of my members who were going to get up and talk into the microphone to kick things off and get people thinking about what they could chat about. I selected some of my members with diverse experiences I thought would be relevant, like going to community college or joining the military to be able to pay for college. Then I remembered that a lot of these kids were thinking about studying music in college because they had come to love music through this nonprofit. So I stood up and said a few sentences into the microphone about what it was like to study music in college, and then I leaned into the microphone and said, "Okay, go," and I signaled to everyone to start mingling.

Shortly after sitting down to talk with one boy who was at my feet, another boy came running across the courtyard toward me. He was tall and skinny, with dreadlocks flying behind him. As he reached me, he practically yelled, "Hi, my name is Anthony, and I never thought I was going to go to college; but then I discovered music, and now I want to go to college—but only if I can study music in college. And I heard you say that you studied music in college, and I have a lot of questions for you—like how many pieces do I have to take to a college music audition? And if I get into a college music program, how many pieces do I have to learn every month?" He barely stopped to breathe, that's how excited he was.

When we can let go of the plan,
we can get what's coming to us. And
oftentimes it's what we wanted all along.

Anthony and I bonded that night, talking about college music programs and his options for standing out at auditions. He started coming over to our house once a week to work on his college essays and applications. After a few months, he started coming over twice a week so my husband and I could spend one evening working on his applications and another night going to an SAT tutor we'd offered to get for him so he could raise his scores.

By that summer, Anthony was spending some nights over at our house, and by the fall he had asked us to take him to college and attend the parent orientation while he went to the student orientation. And when we hugged him goodbye in his dorm room, he said, "Bye, Mom. Bye, Dad. I love you. Are you coming back for parents' weekend?"

I wish I had known that night when he had run up to me with his arm outstretched and his excitement overflowing that Anthony was going to be my son.

It's not what I expected parenthood to look like. I had planned on pregnancy, and childbirth, and a blond-haired, blue-eyed baby who needed to be rocked to sleep. I never thought I'd fast-forward right to driver's ed and the sex talk! But Anthony is my son. He's the son I was supposed to have, the son who was waiting for me to find him, even while I was grieving the path to parenthood that all my friends had taken.

It's normal to cling to the plan. But when we can let go of it, we can get what's coming to us. And oftentimes it's what we wanted all along.

How to Get Comfortable with Changing Plans

If your goal is to reframe unexpected situations so you don't feel as much resentment, there are several ways you can get more comfortable with revising your plan.

Strategy 1: Keep a List of Disappointments-Turned-Positives

First, start keeping a list of things that were disappointing at the time but turned out in your favor. Did you not get into your first-choice college but ended up meeting your best friend or finding your perfect career at your second-choice school? Did you get rejected from your "dream job," only to later land a role that gave you the experience you needed to get where you are today? What about your first crush? Maybe you were devastated when they weren't that into you, or they broke your heart, but you can't imagine life today without your current partner. So many things in life aren't what we would have chosen, but we can reframe them. Looking at life with a fresh perspective, it's easier to see that every upsetting "loss" brings with it some other wins.

Are you being forced to change or are you being called to change?

Strategy 2: Create a Counterintuitive Habit

After you start that list, I recommend creating a new habit that forces you to do something basic in a different way than you're used to doing it. In my life, I've tried to incorporate regular, small changes into my routine. I once heard that brushing your teeth with your nondominant hand can help keep your brain young, and it started me on a crusade to be more open to new ways of doing daily tasks. Start brushing your teeth with the wrong hand like me, or sit in a different seat at the dining table, or take a new street on your daily walk around the block.

When you get comfortable with those little changes, you'll be more open to the larger changes that life sometimes requires. You won't be a stuck-in-your-ways kind of person, because you've built a tolerance to change to make it less painful. Then, when life calls on you to REALLY shake things up, you won't feel so compelled to cling to the way you've always done things. You'll be able to move beyond your comfort zone more easily to seize the opportunity within the altered path.

No one gets through this life without facing change. But the question is, are you being forced to change or are you being called to change? When you reframe your moments of change as a chance to reach your goals in new ways, it won't be so painful to let go of those old plans. Once you've let go, you're ready to move on to the next stage of ReVisionary Thinking: Think Up.

PART 2

THINK UP

Chapter 4

The Enemy of Creative Problem-Solving

"I can't understand why people are frightened of new ideas. I'm frightened of the old ones."—John Cage

*A*re you good at solving problems? Do you get things done in a fast and efficient manner?

Time is an important commodity in today's busy world. Especially in the professional world, there never seems to be enough time. Getting work done faster is a common request of managers everywhere. To understand just how much value society places on speed, you need only look at job descriptions that companies post when they're hiring:

"Fast-paced environment."

"Looking for someone action-oriented."

"Need to work quickly and independently."

The faster you work, the assumption seems to be, the more you'll complete. And the more work you complete, the better.

So do you think you're good at solving problems quickly?

Here's a little exercise for you to try—see how well and how quickly you can accomplish it. All you'll need is a pen or pencil to write in the blank space below the directions.

The Directions Quiz

Directions: Read through ALL the numbered steps below before you begin. Read the directions carefully and do exactly what they say.

1) Use the blank space to the right to complete steps 2–12.

2) Write your first name on the sixth line.

3) Draw a heart above your name.

4) Write your last name in the bottom right corner.

5) Cross out your last name with two lines.

6) Draw a picture of your favorite food underneath your name.

7) Draw a smiley face inside the heart you drew above your first name.

8) Multiply 703 by 66 and write the answer in the bottom left corner.

9) If you have followed the directions carefully to this point, write "I HAVE" in block letters on the first line.

10) Connect your first name and your last name with a squiggly line.

11) Circle all even numbers in the directions.

12) Now that you have finished reading all the instructions, do not do steps 1–11. Leave the space to the right blank.

_____

_____

_____

_____

_____

_____

_____

_____

_____

_____

Did you catch it? Or did you fall for it? When I first encountered this exercise in school, I fell for the trap. I got to direction #12 and couldn't believe my mistake. I always prided myself on being a fast worker, among the first to finish any assignment. I'm a get-it-done kind of person. And sometimes, that's a good thing. But sometimes it isn't, like in the example above.

Snap an image of this page and tag me on Facebook at @CourtneyClarkSpeaker. I'd love to see how you did (and if you did the same thing that second-grade me did)!

"Action bias" is the feeling of being compelled to act quickly and solve a problem, and it's a common impulse. Psychologists think it happens in order to regain a sense of control over a situation. There's a cultural conditioning that can occur, where we learn as children to prefer taking action over waiting, because waiting could be interpreted as "laziness" or "indecisiveness." So action bias isn't just internal—there's a lot of societal pressure to take action. In some cases, we can even be rewarded tangibly for being the kind of person who leaps into action and solves problems quickly, with promotions, raises, or awards.

But there's a flipside to action bias. When we're prone to jumping straight to action, we might not spend enough time thinking about our options before we make a decision. We might not spend enough time gathering ideas before we act. So we move quickly, but we risk moving quickly in the wrong direction. We leap into problem-solving mode before understanding and exploring our options.[1]

When we Think Up, we're going to learn ways to generate ideas and options that can take us forward on successful new paths. And the first step in creating those options is to slow down and avoid action bias.

If you can avoid the traps that push you into moving too quickly, you're likely to be more successful at creating your new plan. For example, research shows that asking "how"-type questions too quickly—like "How am I going to solve this problem?" or "How are we going to address this issue?"—can in fact curb creativity.[2] We're going to need all the creativity we can get when we start to revise our path.

Asking "how" too quickly
can curb creativity.

72

Remember in chapter 2 the discussion about "going with your gut"? Going with your gut can provide the right guidance if you're facing a situation you've faced before. But when you're in an uncertain environment, making choices you've never made before, going with your gut isn't a good strategy.

This is your opportunity to make better choices. Instead of going with your gut or defaulting to taking quick action, you need to move slowly. When you're revising your life plan after you've been knocked off track, it's best to pause, scrutinize your impulses, and open your mind to new possibilities.

To sidestep action bias, you need to invest some time into coming up with new options and solutions. This process is called "divergent thinking." We're going to talk more about the how-tos of divergent thinking and idea generation in the next chapter, but first you need to create an environment where that creativity can happen. To do that, you need to recognize all the factors that may be driving you to take action too quickly, before you've had time to do the work of generating ideas.

The Unconscious Push: Fear

In 2020, membership associations across the world struggled to adapt to the realities of the COVID-19 global pandemic. Association participation had already been lagging in many industries for several years, and now with members' incomes threatened and no ability to host the large conference gatherings that had been a selling point for many members, association leaders found themselves at a crossroads. How would they survive? How would they remain relevant to their members and conference attendees?

Kris Inman is the executive director of the Real Estate Educators Association. In the spring of 2020 when COVID hit, she realized that their upcoming June conference needed to be reimagined. Worried that canceled events would mean a loss of revenue that would force them to close their doors, many of her counterparts at other associations were quickly transitioning to virtual conferences. On the other hand, Inman recognized that a haphazardly thrown together virtual conference would lead to disgruntled members, which might in turn result in canceled memberships. Everywhere she looked, Inman saw her fellow association colleagues making tough decisions that were costing thousands and risking everything.

Inman knew she needed to act fast. But before she pulled the trigger on rebuilding their planned conference in a virtual format, she paused for a moment. She had the realization that she didn't have to create a virtual conference like all her colleagues were doing, just because it was the safe path. Instead of replanning the entire conference herself as a virtual offering and announcing it to the membership, she had another option. She could hear from the members. She could ask what they wanted.

Inman and her team sent out an email survey to their members. The email asked, "How can we help you? How can we best serve you in the current environment?" and the responses flooded in. The REEA team sorted responses into three categories: 1) We already provide that offering and just need to direct the members to those resources, 2) That's out of our scope, and 3) We can help!

The REEA staff, with Inman at the helm, got to work on category 3—We can help! They pooled all the requests that they knew they could address and realized that what they would be able to provide was far more than their usual two-day conference. They could create an entire virtual conference series that lasted for four months. Reflecting on this new path, Inman said, "Instead of two days in person, it was a four-month conference online with one session every day. This let our membership attend virtually when they could, and if they weren't available to attend, we recorded all sessions to view at their convenience."

The payoff of this reimagined event was massive for REEA. Many association conferences lost money in 2020, but not REEA. "Our net was above what we had budgeted for our conference," Inman reports. "This helped us stay alive during the pandemic when so many others suffered." Instead of jumping to a solution, they gathered ideas (more on how to do that and why REAA was so successful in chapter 10). The urge to act quickly was strong, but by taking the time to consult their members, Inman and REEA created something better out of the ashes of the 2020 conference.

Fear can be a potent motivator for people to default to solution mode. You may not want to feel the discomfort of uncertainty for any longer than necessary, so you quickly decide on a course of action. Action is comforting. Action makes you feel in control again. But like Inman and the REEA team discovered, if you're willing to press pause before implementing the first solution that jumps to mind, you're more likely to end up with the *right* solution.

The Unconscious Push: Peer Pressure

If you thought peer pressure was just for children, you might be surprised to learn that adults can fall victim to the influence of doing what everyone else is doing.

Alex had just joined the board of directors of a local nonprofit in his community. He was honored to be able to give input and guidance about a cause that was important to him. Plus, the other people on the board were high-ranking, well-known members of the community, so he felt a sense of pride at being invited to join them. At Alex's first board meeting, he mostly stayed quiet and listened to the conversation around him. He didn't know a lot of the background on the issues being discussed, so he took notes and tried to catch up.

At his second meeting, Alex felt like he had a better understanding of the issues the board was discussing. He raised his hand and asked some questions, and the other board members clarified. Alex started to feel like he was getting the hang of being a board member. But then the discussion turned to a hot topic. The organization was being asked to put out a statement on a divisive issue. The board president, another volunteer just like Alex, explained the situation to the board. Alex braced himself for a heated debate.

But the debate never came. After introducing the issue, the board president said, "The executive director and I have talked about it, and we think the statement outlined here is the best course of action. If everyone agrees, I'll issue a press release with all your names on it tomorrow." The board members looked down at the statement, many nodding their heads while they read. As soon as they finished reading, the board president called for a vote. Alex looked around the room as the board members muttered "aye" and the vote passed without any conversation.

What Alex witnessed is called "premature consensus." Premature consensus happens when nobody speaks up in disagreement, so agreement is assumed. Sometimes premature consensus happens because the people involved are simply bored. If you've ever been in a meeting where people have been sitting there for a while and their eyes start to glaze over, you've witnessed this. People stop caring and just let those in charge have their way.

Another factor that can lead to premature consensus is feeling too deferential to other members of the group. Sometimes if there's a strong leader, that leader can steamroll other people's thoughts or not ever ask for input, like what happened to Alex. People sitting around the table may be thinking, *Well, I'm not totally in agreement with what she is saying. But as the board chair, she probably knows more about the history of this project than I do, so I'm probably fine with whatever she wants to do. It doesn't matter.*

If you're making a decision with other people, try to avoid the trap of premature consensus. Premature consensus is the kind of behavior that can make people feel good in the short term because it avoids conflict, but it leads to problematic decisions in the long run. Remember that making important decisions—especially in new and changing circumstances—is *supposed* to be difficult. It's supposed to include lots of back and forth—and even disagreement.

Premature consensus feels good in the short term
but leads to problematic decisions in the long run.
Remember: disagreement is productive.

And if you're making the decision alone, it's okay to get others to weigh in, but not if you're going to defer to their judgment over your own. If someone in your life has a strong opinion on your decision, it can feel tempting to concede to their preference. You can tell yourself, *They have my best interests at heart. If they think this is the right move, maybe they know something I don't. Maybe I'm not seeing the situation clearly enough because I'm too close to it.* Those are all important points to consider, and getting a second opinion is usually helpful (more on that in part 3). But there's a difference between asking for advice and surrendering your decision-making responsibilities to another person. Don't let someone else rush you into a decision when the consequences are yours to live with.

Problem First, Solution Second

If you decide to take a pause instead of jumping to action, you might feel adrift. You might feel like slowing down at a critical time in your life is a mistake. It's natural for us as humans to feel a need to do *something*. So what should you do, if not jump right into solving the problem?

This pause is the perfect time to define the problem. What's actually the issue here? Is the current situation the source of the pain, or is it just a symptom of a bigger problem? When did this start? Are there other, unsolved issues contributing to this problem and making it worse? Would solving those problems allow for an easier solution to the current issue?

Teasing apart the elements related to a single problem is difficult. That's why many people skip it. But defining the problem is what experienced problems-solvers do. One 1994 study on problem-solving showed that experts in any given field spend more time defining problems than new employees, who jump directly to problem-solving.[3] So attempting to solve a problem before defining it is a newbie mistake. Real experts, the people whose capability is trusted on an issue, would never risk solving an unclear problem.

I got stuck solving the wrong problem once. When I got engaged to my husband, I was embarrassed about my cooking skills. I had scorched only three pans beyond saving, but that was two more than I felt good about. (Oh, I also set a toaster oven on fire once. But that was in college, so I'd like to think that won't happen again.)

When I reached my thirties, I had definitely gotten better at cooking. But my food was just...okay. I was practicing all the time—I worked fewer hours than my husband, who was my fiancé at the time, so I'd pull out the *Cooking Light* magazine, find a recipe, and cook us dinner most nights. He'd cook about once a week, and his food was just better than mine. Significantly better. He was confident in the kitchen, and his food was so full of flavor.

I decided I needed to improve faster. I joined cooking classes at Williams Sonoma, and I learned how to roast a chicken. I watched Food Network. I practiced my knife skills and worked on getting comfortable with when meat was fully cooked. I became more skilled at timing dishes so they'd all be done at the same time. I was getting a little better. And then my husband and I went on our honeymoon.

We ended up in Italy, where I ate what felt like five meals a day, four of which were pasta. Our first Sunday back after we returned from Rome, we were grocery shopping. There, at the checkout, was a copy of *Gourmet Magazine*: "The Pasta Issue." And the photo on the cover was of penne salsiccia, which I'd had a LOT of in Italy. I threw that magazine down on the conveyor belt and committed to reading it cover to cover.

The following Sunday, we were back at the grocery store. This time, I was armed with a shopping list that included ALL of the ingredients for that delicious penne salsiccia from the cover of *Gourmet Magazine*. As I prowled through the store, I heard my newlywed husband behind me go, "Uh, Courtney? Heavy whipping cream? Butter? Sausage? Is this from *Cooking Light*?"

"No, it's from that gourmet magazine I bought, with recipes for dishes like we had in Italy! I'm going to make penne salsiccia tonight. I can't wait!" I responded.

6:00 P.M. I'm starting dinner. This recipe calls for VERY expensive, very fragile threads of saffron to be soaked in water. I'm trying not to panic.

6:28. I'm trying not to scald the heavy whipping cream in the pan.

6:47. I'm trying not to overcook the pasta.

6:52. I carry the plates out to the table. I set them down with a deep breath. For a moment I consider letting my husband take the first bite and tell me what he thinks, but then I think FORGET THAT. THIS WAS MY IDEA. I MADE THIS MEAL. I put the bite in my mouth, and I turn to my husband in shock.

I can't believe what I'm tasting.

"I don't stink at cooking! *Cooking Light* must stink at cooking! Because I. am. AMAZING!" I would have said more, but I needed to use my mouth for the important work of eating my phenomenal pasta.

Here's what I realized: I had been using low-fat materials and expecting restaurant-quality results. No shade to *Cooking Light*, but there's a reason full-fat food tastes better. My cooking issue was simply a materials problem. But I had been trying for over a year to solve it with more SKILLS training. No wonder it wasn't working! You can't solve a materials problem with more skills training.

Has anything like that ever happened to you, either at home or at work? You know there's a problem, so you leap to solve it. But if you aren't solving the *right* problem, you're not solving the problem at all.

If you're not solving the right problem,
you're not solving the problem at all.

To Solve the Right Problems, Get Out of the Tunnel

Every one of us knows only what we know. And we don't know what we don't know. That sounds obvious. But too often we make decisions based solely on our limited knowledge, without ever digging for more information. I call this limited knowledge "the Tunnel."

Tunnel vision happens when we assume that our experiences and knowledge provide enough information to make smart decisions. And sometimes they do! But as we talked about—the more novel your situation and the more uncertain your path, the less likely you are to have the know-how you need to proceed. Tunnel vision is a result of denying how much there is you don't know and taking action based on only a small sliver of knowledge.

We all get tunnel vision sometimes. But if your goal is to start solving problems in your life with as little pain as possible, you want to solve the right problems the first time and not waste time trying solutions that won't work. So you want to gather information on the front end and be sure that you're solving the right problems, with the right tools, at the right time. To do that, you have to get out of the Tunnel.

Time is, of course, one of the most important things you can give yourself to get out of the Tunnel. In the next several chapters, you'll learn more ways to boost your creativity and see your path ahead from different angles. But if you don't start by giving yourself time, you won't get the answers you need. Study after study of creative problem-solving shows that a lack of time is one of the key elements that keeps individuals and teams from addressing problems correctly and coming up with smart solutions.[4]

Conserving time and moving fast seems like a smart move, especially when it's crunch time. But what if taking a small amount of time would yield wildly superior results? Would that be worth it?

That's a question that Toshiba asked themselves. A Japanese manufacturing company, Toshiba is widely known for their consumer electronics products. Leaders at Toshiba have always striven to produce top-quality devices, so they hire exceptional engineers and designers to build their products. But they realized they could do even better.

Toshiba embraced the idea of helping their employees escape tunnel vision. They developed one of the most unique training programs for their engineers and designers in the industry. If you get hired as an engineer or a designer at Toshiba, you don't start your first day of work as an engineer or a designer. First, you start by reporting to the customer service department. You spend weeks answering customer service calls: "This button doesn't work," "This doesn't make sense," "I can't figure out how to get this operation to happen." You begin to learn the features of your products that cause customers to struggle. You learn what they don't understand. You learn what keeps breaking. You learn what frustrates the customer about Toshiba products.

Then, you move into the sales department. You spend another several weeks talking to potential customers considering your product or another product. "What features are they looking for?" "What's most important to them?" "What's a deal breaker?" You learn how your prospective customers are making their decisions. You learn what features the marketplace values. You learn what people think is worth paying for and what they don't care about.

Then—after months in customer service and sales—and only then, do you get to start designing and building products for Toshiba. When you start your work as a designer, you have a much broader understanding of what your clients need and want. You aren't engineering products based on your assumptions about what will work. You've done the research. You've answered the questions. You've broken out of the Tunnel.

If you want to see something different, try DOING something different—just like they do at Toshiba. Get outside of your day-to-day and start gathering data like a scientist. Taking a pause before jumping into problem-solving mode isn't being lazy. It's the way you ensure that your next steps will be the right steps.

If you want to see something different,
try DOING something different.

Remember: Taking action too quickly is the enemy of creative problem-solving. Before you start to prepare for your new plan, take the time to sidestep your action bias and break out of your tunnel vision.

Committing to a great idea with a faulty plan would be committing to failure. Give yourself permission to make your next plan the right plan, and you'll get where you want to go.

Chapter 5

Creating Space for Choices

"After you've done a thing the same way for two years, look it over carefully. After five years, look at it with suspicion. After ten years, throw it all away and start over."—Alfred Edward Perlman

*H*ow many choices have you made in your life? The answer could be millions. We make dozens of choices a day. Decaf coffee or regular this morning? The blue shirt or the green one? Take the highway or the surface roads? Pick up the phone or send an email?

Then there are the bigger choices: correct your boss and risk an argument or let it go? Stay in this relationship or end it? Have children or don't?

When we select one option over another, we refer to it as "making a choice." But what most people don't realize is that we actually engage in a process of *making* choices. We create them. We don't just pick them; we construct them.

While you make large and small choices every day, the decision-making process is never more crucial than when you've hit a roadblock and you're planning what to do next. The choices you make at these critical junctures can change your entire life. For that reason,

ReVisionary Thinking requires that you pay special attention at this stage so that you can come up with the strongest options for your path forward.

We don't just pick choices—
we construct them.

The process of coming up with these choices is scientifically called "idea generation" or "option generation," although most of us just call it "brainstorming." Brainstorming is an important part of how we plan our biggest choices, but we often skip over it or rush through it because it takes time. This is why we learned to avoid action bias in the last chapter—so that we could take the time we need for brainstorming—because making the *best* choice almost always involves having lots of options from which to choose. Brainstorming is where the real promise of crafting and revising your new plan happens.

Creating possibilities at this stage serves an important role: having options gives you an increased sense of power. Facing change can make you feel like your power has been taken away. And in many cases, it has! Prior to a big change, you may have had everything set up to your advantage. You knew how to be successful. You knew how to get your job done. You knew what you needed in order to be happy. And now the goalposts have moved, and you have to find your way back to being successful again. Everything is harder.

If you had only a single choice in a situation like that, it wouldn't feel much like a choice. It might feel like you were being forced into a decision you didn't pick, which could lead to resentment down the line. But if you have a menu of several options from which to choose, you can feel a sense of power returning. Even if some of your options aren't very good ones, they serve a purpose: they provide you with agency. It's important to be able to say, "That's a terrible choice! I reject that choice!" Even in the rejection of a choice, your personal power starts to build up, little by little. You may not have been in control of the change, but you are in control of the choice.

You may not have been in control of the change, but you are in control of the choice.

Brainstorm Better

If brainstorming plays such a critical role in making solid choices for our work and our lives, how has it developed a poor reputation over the years? Why do so many people cringe at the thought of brainstorming? Much of the current negativity toward brainstorming can likely be traced back to how badly brainstorming has been misinterpreted over the years.

Have you ever played the childhood game "telephone"? In this game, a bunch of people sit in a circle shoulder to shoulder. One person starts off the game by whispering a sentence to the person on their right. That person whispers the sentence to the person on THEIR right, and the sentence travels around the circle, quietly whispered, until it reaches the last person in the circle. The last person in the circle announces the phrase they heard, and the group gets to see if the message is still the same as when the leader started it or if the message degraded through repeated mishearings. In most cases, the message gets jumbled along the way.

That's what happened with brainstorming. The way most individuals and organizations practice brainstorming looks nothing like what its originator, Alex Osborn, recommended in 1953. So if you dislike the practice of brainstorming, it's possible that you haven't been doing it correctly in the first place. The best practices for brainstorming don't take long; they simply take a small amount of patience.

Go Long

Brainstorming is supposed to take time. Good options don't just *come* to you as though a little idea fairy tapped you on the head right before you exclaimed, "Aha!" Yet most brainstorming sessions, both in work and individual settings, don't take enough time. When Osborn went back to organizations more than 25 years after releasing his findings on brainstorming best practices, he found that the average group brainstorming session was 20 minutes or less, leading him to conclude that the groups weren't spending enough time generating options.[1]

Studies have shown that when groups and individuals are attempting to come up with creative solutions, the longer they work at it, the better the solutions become. Early ideas aren't as creative as later ideas. Therefore, if we don't brainstorm long enough, we fail to break what I call "the Boring Barrier" and instead are stuck with ideas that are close to the status quo.

To brainstorm correctly, allot more time than you think might be necessary so you don't feel crunched to settle for the first decent idea that springs to mind.

Do More

Breaking the Boring Barrier doesn't have to mean a single long session. In fact, doing several short- to- mid-length sessions can be even better than one long brainstorming session.

Google is known for being at the top of the innovation game. "Thinking like a Googler" has become shorthand for generating creative—even mind-blowing—solutions to problems. One strategy that Google uses to maximize each employee's creative ability is to invite them to brainstorm in several different ways over many days. After gathering as a group to frame the problem, Google employees typically are sent off on their own to generate ideas individually. The individual team members then reconvene and share their ideas in a team session. While the group is together, they build on each other's ideas, adding their knowledge or asking questions to flesh out the other person's concept.

There are several benefits to having groups brainstorm the same problem in various settings: in large groups, small groups, individually, and one on one. Conversation around ideas can happen very differently when the idea's owner is speaking to one person instead of 20. Having different opportunities to flesh out the explanation in different-size groups helps strengthen the concept.

Most importantly, everyone processes new ideas differently. People who identify as extroverts, for example, do a lot of their processing verbally. Extroverts can dominate group brainstorming sessions because they often feel comfortable talking about an idea as soon as it pops into their head. Introverts, on the other hand, tend to need more time to process an idea internally before they feel comfortable sharing it. They may not speak up in a large group setting. When you give introverts solo time to brainstorm before asking for their input, you're more likely to get them to participate. If the goal of brainstorming is to get everyone's ideas out on the table, you want to include both extroverts and introverts, and having multiple sessions of different sizes is the best way to do that.

If you're brainstorming solo, you won't be able to change up your group size, but you can still get the benefit of committing to several, shorter sessions rather than trying to come up with all your best ideas at once. Doing so will make it even easier to follow the next two guidelines, as well.

Change It Up

Do you always work at your desk? When you have big family conversations, do you have a favorite chair? When you go to the conference room for a meeting, do you usually sit in the same seat? Most of us are creatures of habit, and we tend to follow a routine without even realizing it. But that routine could be stifling our creativity.

Outside influences like what you see, hear, and feel can have an impact on whether your brain is in creative mode or uninspired mode. Sitting in the same seat at the conference table or the same spot on the sofa can lead to the same old thought patterns. When you're trying to come up with new solutions, your brain needs variety. Change up your location and surroundings. Take a walk outside to do your thinking today, or go to a new coffee shop.

It's also a good idea to look at other elements of your life or work that could be contributing to a "stuck" thought pattern. Consider having conversations with new people. In a typical day, many of us talk with the same people over and over again, day after day. You catch up with your family over breakfast. You chat with your colleagues. You have lunch with the same person frequently. Often those conversations are easy because you're familiar with the person. You know what they think about current events. You can almost predict their perspective on many issues. But talking with a new person might just allow you to look at an issue in a new way. It might force you to clarify an opinion you hold that hasn't been challenged before. Talking to someone new is a way to make a small shift, but it could dramatically influence your ability to think differently and be innovative.

Turn Off

Do you have a preferred time of day? Are you an early bird or a night owl? It's common to feel a preference for a specific time of day you feel most productive. You may even have been encouraged to arrange your schedule around "your" time of the day. But don't go scheduling brainstorming time during your most productive time of day, or you may be disappointed.

The time of day you feel most productive is the time your brain is most successful at linear, logical tasks. In this "flow state," you'll be able to move from task to task easily, acting sequentially and solving familiar problems. But creativity requires the opposite of linear thinking. Creativity calls for establishing connections between seemingly unrelated ideas. It draws on intuition and artistry more than concrete facts.

To tap into your creative mindset, try brainstorming at the opposite time of day to whenever you feel most productive. When your brain is in "off" mode, like when you feel a little drowsy or restless, or when you're focusing on something else, your brain is less linear and more likely to make those creative connections. It's the reason many people joke about having "aha!" moments in the shower—they aren't trying to be productive, so their thoughts are free to pinball around. To boost your brainstorming power, schedule idea generation for a time you don't need to be in productive mode.

Becoming an "Idea Person"

Some people are naturally good at brainstorming possibilities. You'll hear someone like this referred to as "an idea person," especially in the workplace. "Oh, he's a real idea person" usually means you can trust him to generate innovative solutions to new problems and have a fresh take on old problems.

How does an idea person become an idea person? Usually, idea people are also proactive problem-solvers. An idea person can see the good in the status quo but also notice the holes. They see what could be improved instead of just enjoying "the way we've always done it." To become more of an idea person, start looking at your environment for opportunities for improvement.

New Language, New Perspective

Even changing something as minor as the language we use in reference to our environment can make a significant difference.

Nobody cares about language and understands the importance of word choice more than television writers. Writing an episode of television comedy is about as creative a job as anyone could do. The writers who do the work are committed to innovative, fresh storylines. Yet often the environment where the work is performed is very similar from show to show.

Mike Schur, the TV producer and writer behind hits like *Parks and Recreation*, *Brooklyn Nine-Nine*, and *The Good Place*, doesn't build his writers' rooms the same way other showrunners do. One of the most unique elements of his writers' room is something called "the Candy Bag." The Candy Bag takes the place of what other writers' rooms would call "the trash." In a typical TV writers' room, writers generate hundreds of ideas, only a fraction of which will ever make it into the half-hour show. The ideas that get cut typically go into the trash—but not in a Mike Schur writers' room.

If you write for a Mike Schur show and your joke gets cut, it goes into the Candy Bag. Writers who work with Schur joke that the phrase "Candy Bag" just feels emotionally better than "the trash." Your joke is already getting cut out of the show's script—you don't need to be reminded that it's garbage. But Schur does more than just change the name to make the trash sound less hurtful. He also saves the contents of the Candy Bag. When the episode is being filmed, the episode's head writer has the Candy Bag on set, and they can pull from the document to do reshoots and try out alternate jokes.

Schur realized that the typical way of working—throwing ideas into the trash when they didn't seem valuable enough to keep—wasn't helping his writers produce their most creative work. By changing the language used, Schur changed the environment on his sets to allow his writers to freely share ideas and not feel like they might be classified as garbage.

Words matter. The language you use matters. If you say, "I've hit a dead end," then you'll find you've hit a dead end. Notice your language, your habits, and how they influence your thoughts. Are your thoughts helping you become an idea person? Or are they keeping you locked into the status quo?

Getting Better with Age

The length of time you've been in your career can also influence whether or not you feel like an idea person at work. When I conducted my research across the United States, I was surprised to find that mid-career and late-career employees seem to be the most able to generate novel ideas and possible solutions to a given problem. Going into the study, I expected to find the opposite: I expected that the longer someone had been in their role, the less able they would be to come up with creative ideas to move forward, based on the findings that seasoned employees seemed less willing to let go of "the way we've always done it." But the research showed something interesting: once they got on board with changing their plans, older employees reported a willingness to find more options to solve problems before giving up, compared to younger employees. The reason for the disparity seems to be that newer employees—those with less than two years of experience or between two and five years of experience—said they didn't feel confident that they would be able to find creative solutions to problems.[2]

So experience, it seems, can breed creativity. With experience and enough information, you can feel confident about generating new ideas and thinking up possibilities for the future. The key is to keep tapping into opportunities for improvement, instead of seeking comfort in the way things have always been done.

If you're a newer employee, take heart. While you may still be gaining the experience of your more seasoned peers, you can find other ways to strengthen your creative muscles. Spend time on the four guidelines suggested in the "Brainstorm Better" section earlier in this chapter. Look to your older colleagues for guidance and patience when you feel eager to jump ahead to a solution. With practice and time, you'll have all the tools you need to generate plenty of solutions for the problems that lie ahead.

Cultivate Curiosity

As a child, you may have been told "curiosity killed the cat" if you asked too many questions. But curiosity is the path to knowledge, and knowledge leads to wisdom. To become a more creative and open-minded person, it helps to develop a sense of curiosity.

Remember the concept of "beginner's mind" from chapter 2? A curious person doesn't think to themselves, *I know the answer. I'm certain how this will turn out.* A curious person thinks, *I wonder how this works. I wonder what the variables are. I wonder how I could impact what's happening.*

Certainty is a compelling trait in a person. It inspires trust and confidence. But if a situation is inherently uncertain, then a person acting with certainty is not contributing productively to creating a positive outcome. Instead of pretending to be certain or following a leader who is pretending to be certain, take the time to get curious about your options.

Take the time to get curious about your options.

Enough Is Enough

Sometimes people hesitate to make the changes they need to make to their plan because they approach innovation as an all-or-nothing endeavor. They feel like creativity is worthwhile only if it involves changing every aspect of a plan and coming up with something entirely new—something so big it must be groundbreaking—rather than considering smaller tweaks that can have big payoffs. But this approach to innovation can stall, rather than inspire, improvement. Oftentimes the most generative creativity comes from knowing when enough change is enough.

Kendall and John Antonelli run a small cheese shop in Austin, Texas. The store, Antonelli's Cheese Shop, opened in 2010 as a tiny storefront with three employees (two of the three were Kendall and John themselves). As the store grew, so did Kendall and John's family. They were running the shop, raising two small children, and building out a wholesale business for the company, as well.

Their goal for Antonelli's Cheese Shop was starting to become a reality. The shop became like a specialized grocery store: cheese lovers could come in and get taken on a tour by their cheesemongers (they're like the wine sommeliers of the cheese world), finding just the right cheese to pair with any food or wine. A large aspect of making the store part of the community was the cheese-tasting events hosted there. Antonelli's would put together delicious wine and cheese pairings, making for a delicious date night experience where you could buy more of your favorites to take home for later.

And then COVID-19 hit. With the shelter-in-place order in Austin, small businesses like Antonelli's Cheese Shop started dying off by the dozens. As a grocery store, Kendall and John were allowed to keep the business OPEN, but customers were not allowed to enter the small space. Without being allowed inside, an entire piece of the Antonelli's Cheese Shop experience was missing. The whole reason you might buy your cheese at Antonelli's and not the big-name grocery store is because you want the experience. You want a unique cheese. You want someone to tell you what makes it so special, and you probably want to sample it.

But none of that was possible. So Kendall and John pivoted, like many small businesses. But they didn't pivot just once. It was their combined series of smart adaptations that helped them stay afloat.

First, Kendall and John offered curbside pickup, like many food purveyors and retailers. But they knew that didn't provide their loyal customers with the Antonelli's experience they had come to love. So they created a virtual cheesemonger option: their cheesemongers— these cheese connoisseurs—would take customers through the shop virtually on an iPad. No, the customers couldn't TASTE the cheese, but they could do everything else. The cheesemonger could show you the color. They could slice or snap it for you so you could see just how firm or soft it was. They could compare it to the flavor and texture of a similar cheese. They could prepare an entire cheese board for you (Google the pandemic cheese board trend—it was a thing!). It was survival mode, and it was working.

They had made cheese shopping virtual, but they were ready to go to the next level. Kendall and John decided that they could take their wine and cheese pairing events virtual, too. They prepared the cheese, just like usual. They paired the wine, just like usual. Then they took to Facebook. They started spreading the word about their "virtual cheese-tasting parties" on Facebook Live. Customers could place their orders for a cheese platter for however many people they wanted to serve; then, at any time during the day of the event, the customers would swing by Antonelli's for contactless curbside delivery.

At 6:30 P.M., the Facebook Live began. Kendall and John appeared, sheltered in their own home, at their dining room table. Their kids were nearby, munching on cheese and crackers. They walked you through everything you were tasting. They explained why this cheese had this undertone but this one didn't. They explained the origins, the milk percentage, the perfect nibbles to eat between bites of cheese. They explained why the wine paired perfectly. Just like they would do if you were in their shop at an in-person event.

And if you hadn't purchased a cheese board in advance? If you hadn't heard that Antonelli's was doing virtual cheese tastings? You'd be scrolling Facebook and see three of your friends watching the Facebook Live, eating their cheese, and commenting. You'd feel left out. You couldn't physically be WITH your friends, but you wanted to be doing something together with them. You'd log on to Antonelli's website to try to get a cheese board for the next day, but you'd see that the virtual tasting parties sold out two weeks in advance every single time.

Kendall and John Antonelli took something they've always done and changed the delivery mechanism. But they didn't just "go virtual" like everyone did in the early days of the pandemic. They broadened the reach. They put it on live social media. They leaned into the sense of community that we were all missing. By changing the delivery mode, they also changed their audience. They were able to get in front of people who hadn't even known they existed.

And in going virtual, Kendall and John also overcame their own limitations. With virtual cheese tastings, they weren't restricted by the size of their store or the number of chairs they owned. They weren't limited by how many parking spots are in the parking lot. They weren't limited by whether or not you could get a babysitter on a Saturday night to make an in-person event.

Sometimes we miss opportunities to make changes and improvements until we're forced into them. The diagram below shows a way you can start to think about hidden opportunities with a fresh perspective, like Kendall and John did.

Take a look at the diagram below.

The Opportunities Matrix

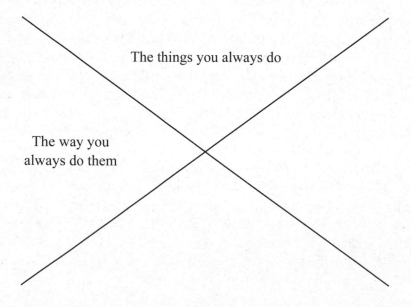

Start in the top quadrant of the diagram, and think about the activities you perform in a day. If you're thinking about your home life, consider your chores, your errands, your self-care routine, your meals. If you're thinking about work, list the reports you run, the meetings you attend, the client calls you have. Then move into the left section and reflect on HOW you perform those tasks. Does this errand always happen on Tuesdays? Does this meeting typically have ten people? Does the client call always take 30 minutes? Is the meeting always face to face?

As you start to think about ways you could break the status quo and find areas for improvement, you have two choices: you can create something completely new from scratch, or you could tweak the existing model. Both quadrants are change. Both quadrants take confidence and commitment and leadership to occupy. One isn't better than the other. One isn't long term and the other short term. They're just two different ways of revising the plan.

The Opportunities Matrix

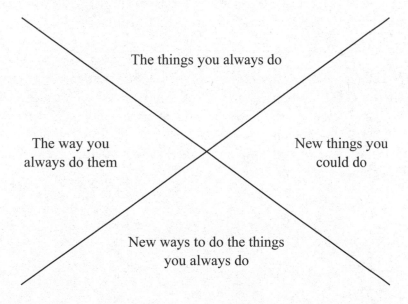

The things you always do

The way you
always do them

New things you
could do

New ways to do the things
you always do

For many of us, when we think of making changes in our work or our personal life, we think of big, sweeping changes. We think about complete overhauls. If something isn't working, we want to throw it out and start over. But the Antonelli's story shows us the power of knowing just how much change is enough. You don't have to change everything to change…everything.

Stop in the Name of Options

"I don't need to take the time to think up a lot of choices. I know what the right thing to do is."

If that's the voice you hear in your head, throw up a red flag and tell that voice to quiet down. Remember what we've talked about in previous chapters: in familiar environments, it's okay to go with your gut. But in novel situations, you may *think* you know the right choice, but you could be wrong. Whether your first idea is the right idea or not, bringing a creative and curious mindset to your problems will only ever be a benefit, never a drawback. When you get curious about your choices, you may find a solution you'd never have considered.

Living your best life consists of making the best choices. How can you make the best choices if you don't have the best menu of choices to select from? When you look at all the options in front of you, that's the moment you realize you're in control. You may not have chosen to be where you are right now, but you get a choice in what comes next.

Meet the ReVisionary

Terri Broussard Williams

Different Jobs, Same Purpose

In high school, Terri Broussard Williams knew she wanted to be a journalist. She started working in television journalism at 16, confident that her mission in life was, as she puts it, "to provide people access to information so they can do good in the world."

After years in the difficult TV news industry, Terri decided she needed a change, and she accepted a job as the press secretary for a US Senate campaign. She felt energized by the shift, but when her candidate lost the race in 2002, she had no idea what to do next. Some friends encouraged her to try political lobbying. "The only lobbyist I knew at the time was Elle Woods from *Legally Blonde 2*," Terri acknowledges, "but the way people described the work to me, I thought I'd be good at it." Terri went back home to Louisiana to work as a lobbyist, and she never lost a single bill the entire time she lobbied in her home state. She felt like she could do that work forever.

But in the past several years, the world has shifted. As a woman of color, Terri felt called to use her skills in a new way. Terri began narrowing her focus to become a social justice lobbyist, advocating for complex policy changes that will lead to greater social equality. And now she is adding a new position to her resume: teaching social justice policy to undergraduate students at Texas A&M University.

Although Terri has changed careers several times, her life story has a common through line. In every role, she is providing people access to information so they can do good in the world.

Chapter 6

Avoiding the
Goldilocks Paradox

*"When the winds of change blow, some people build
walls and others build windmills."*
—Chinese Proverb

*A*fter recovering from cancer and the subsequent divorce at age
26, I had a realization: "Oh. That was my big life challenge,"
I reasoned. "Everybody has to climb a mountain at some point, so
that was my mountain. That's my big life story, right there. I'm a
cancer survivor." That's what I told myself. And that explanation
made sense...right up until I was diagnosed with cancer a second time
two years later. It was early stage, so my oncologist removed it with
surgery, and I got right back to trying to live my life.

If you've ever dealt with a long-term health issue, you know that
doctor's offices can become a source of anxiety. Even if you never
felt nervous around doctors before, once you've gotten bad news a
few times, you can start to feel primed for bad news. In the cancer
world, we call it "scanxiety"—that specific type of worry that crops
up before your regular scans. You fear that this time, the scans will
find something.

When I went to see my oncologist for my five-year follow-up visit, I was excited to celebrate. For many types of cancer, being cancer free for five years is cause for a big celebration, because that's when your survival rates go up and your chances of recurrence go down. Dr. Ross came into my exam room that day and said, "Congratulations, five years cancer free! We can graduate you now. You don't have to come every six months anymore; you only have to come once a year."

I replied, "That's great. I'm happy to graduate. But you know what? You said that at this appointment, for five years today, I was going to get a lot more scans before I graduated." He looked at me questioningly. "You said I was going to get another CT scan. I haven't had one of those in three years. And you were going to schedule a brain MRI. I never had one of those."

"You don't need scans," Dr. Ross replied. "We would do that only if we thought you had metastatic cancer. You don't."

"Oh no, I know that!" I countered. "But you said you wanted to get some baseline scans for my chart, just in case the cancer ever comes back again. Since it's already come back once, you said you wanted baseline scans of what my body looks like right now, so we know what's normal and what's not. Just in case."

He caved. "Okay, we can do baseline scans. That's fine, if that's what you want." Dr. Ross wrote the order for the scans, and I went downstairs to have the tests.

I've learned an important rule about waiting for test results: If the nurse calls with your test results, it's almost always good news. If the doctor calls, it's a good idea to sit down. When I pulled my phone out of my purse after yoga class and heard Dr. Ross's voice on the other end of the line, I just knew—my cancer must be back.

"Courtney, it's Dr. Ross."

My stomach started to churn. "We got your brain MRI back and…" And what? It felt like he was taking hours to say just a few words.

"There's no cancer. It's not cancer."

I nearly dropped the phone. *No cancer.*

"There's no cancer…but…there's an aneurysm in your brain. It's about to hemorrhage. I can't believe we found this. Were you really not having any symptoms? We wouldn't have found this if it hadn't been for your cancer."

I don't remember the drive home from yoga class. My mind was spinning. I'm a cancer survivor. THAT'S my story. THAT'S my big life hurdle. I've already climbed my mountain and survived. This isn't fair.

But I didn't have time to worry about fairness. The cancer hospital doesn't operate on vascular issues, only tumors, so I had to research and find the best neurosurgeon available. I flew to New York City to be seen by the best neurosurgeon I could find. Dr. Solomon had performed more of the type of surgery I would need than anyone else. I got lucky and was able to schedule an appointment with him in just a few weeks.

Sitting in his New York exam room, Dr. Solomon gave me all my options and then walked out of the room to let me consider what I was going to choose. My head was swimming: I could have a craniotomy. I could have gamma knife radiation surgery. I could have two endovascular embolizations and THEN a craniotomy. I could watch and wait and see what happens.

Susan, Dr. Solomon's nurse, came into the room. She sat down and looked at me with compassion.

"Okay, have you had a minute to think about the options Dr. Solomon gave you? Do you know what you're considering?"

"No, Susan. I have no idea. He gave me too many options," I snapped.

Susan leaned forward and put her hand on top of mine. "I know it feels like an overwhelming choice. But he didn't give you too many options. He gave you four options. He does that on purpose. Dr. Solomon discovered that a lot of his colleagues give three options to patients. But he realized that when they do, patients often interpret one option as the conservative option and one as the aggressive or risky option. Then they can automatically default to the middle option without even thinking about it." She leaned back.

"Dr. Solomon discovered that when he gives four options, people consider their choices a lot more. They seem to make better choices."

It felt overwhelming. It felt like too many choices, but Susan assured me it wasn't. Four options, she promised, was an ideal number for the position I found myself in. I sat there with Nurse Susan and considered my options. In the end, I went for the most aggressive choice—two endovascular procedures followed by a full craniotomy. Three brain surgeries in eight days. When I woke up from the craniotomy, even Dr. Solomon was impressed by how few cognitive deficits I had and how smoothly my recovery was starting. This was a situation where there wasn't a single right choice, but the choice I made was a good one for me.

What Would Goldilocks Do?

In the fairy-tale story of "Goldilocks and the Three Bears," a little girl finds herself wandering around the woods. The lost Goldilocks stumbles upon a small cottage and lets herself inside. In the cottage, Goldilocks finds three chairs, and she sits in them. One is too small for her, one is too large for her, but the third chair is just right. She finds three bowls of porridge and eats from them: one is too hot, one is too cold, but the third is just right. After finishing the porridge, Goldilocks feels sleepy and wants to take a nap. She finds the bedroom where one bed is too hard, another is too soft, but the third bed is just right. She lies down to go to sleep in the third bed, where she is discovered by the three bears who live in the cottage.

Goldilocks decided the middle choice was always perfect. The other options were too much: too small, too hot, too hard, too soft. In comparison, the middle choice felt like the "right" choice. Encountering extremes made the middle-ground option feel the most comfortable.

Just like the fictional Goldilocks, when we're given three options, it can feel tempting to default to the choice that lies in the middle. It can feel safe—gut instinct-approved. But as Dr. Solomon warned, just because an option is in the middle doesn't mean it's the correct choice.

The middle-ground option might feel the safest or most comfortable, but it's not always the right choice.

The world often seems to give us three choices to pick from. It's common to be offered the bronze, silver, or gold package when making a purchase. There's a reason we typically encounter three offerings: it's a sales trick. Sales and marketing experts have discovered that by positioning the item they most want to sell in the middle, flanked by two less appealing options, sales will soar. In contrast, having too many purchasing choices makes it more difficult to persuade customers to buy on the spot. So three options is good...*if* you're a salesperson trying to convince people to buy your product. By using the psychological hack marketers call "the rule of three," you can give customers the perception of choice while actually influencing their decision.

But if you aren't a salesperson trying to move a product or service? If you're just a regular person trying to make a decision? Three options may not be enough for you. I call it "the Goldilocks Paradox." We've become used to a world in which three choices is common, but three choices often aren't enough to make a smart decision.

The Goldilocks Paradox becomes a mental trap into which we run the risk of falling. If having three choices feels comfortable to us, we may limit ourselves by considering only three options for moving forward, thinking they're enough. But with three options to choose from, we may find ourselves defaulting toward the option we perceive as being in the middle. We've conditioned ourselves to feel like three options is enough. But that wasn't for *our* benefit—that was a psychological strategy used by salespeople to drive purchases.

The rule of three wasn't meant to serve you. It was meant to sell to you. Why would you use a strategy on yourself meant to offer you the mere illusion of choice? Why would you manipulate yourself with a tactic meant to get you to do what someone ELSE wants you to do? Don't leave your crunch-time decision-making to the rule of three. If you're facing a fork in the road and you have only one or two or even three choices, be careful. Don't fall victim to the Goldilocks Paradox.

Quantity Equals Quality

If having three options doesn't provide the best chance at finding the right choice for your path forward, how many options do you need? It may surprise you to know that the best way to come up with *quality* ideas is to generate a *quantity* of ideas. When it comes to generating new ideas, quantity equals quality.

If that surprises you, you're not alone. Many of us have been taught that quantity and quality exist on two ends of the spectrum: you can either have a quantity of something or you can have a smaller amount but higher quality version of the same thing. You can have one fancy jacket that will last for decades or five polyester jackets from the discount store. You can have a dozen cheeseburgers from the drive-through or one really nice steak dinner.

But life choices aren't cheeseburgers. You can have both quantity AND quality. In fact, the scientists who study how ideas are generated will tell you that the best way to come up with quality ideas is to make sure you have a quantity of options to choose from.[1] When you spend time generating more ideas, you're likely to uncover higher quality ideas.

When it comes to generating new ideas,
quantity equals quality.

Like you learned in chapter 5, your earliest ideas are closest to status quo. Those ideas tend to follow a standard, predictable pattern of thinking.[2] But when you spend more time brainstorming, you run out of obvious solutions. When you've exhausted the run-of-the-mill ideas, you're forced to hunt deeper for new ideas. These new ideas can lead you to new paths that you might never have explored if you hadn't taken the time to consider what other options you could try.

To generate a quantity of options (and therefore quality options), try asking yourself a simple question: "What else?"

I learned the "What else?" trick from my father. Like many children, when I was little I would find myself frustrated when I couldn't get things to turn out the way I expected. And like many children, I would come running to a grown-up to fix it for me.

I started noticing that many of my friends' parents would respond to these moments in one of two ways. Some parents would immediately get involved. They'd take over finishing the homework project or call the parents of another child directly to work it out among the adults. Today, some people refer to those individuals who solve problems for their kids as "helicopter parents." I noticed another set of parents would say, "Handle it yourself," "Work it out among yourselves," or the slightly more supportive but still removed—"You'll figure it out."

My dad didn't do either of those two things. He didn't solve the issue *for* me or steer me back to solve it myself. He investigated the problem *with* me. He would ask me what had happened, but then he followed up with this: "Hmmm…what else have you tried?" I would always wail back, "I've tried everything!"

He'd sit with me patiently. "Oh yeah? You've tried everything? Okay, well what have you tried? What else? Anything else?"

He never came right out and said, "I don't think you've tried everything." He didn't have to. I'd inevitably realize it on my own. The more he asked, "What else?" the more it would become obvious that I hadn't thought of everything. There were still more ways I could solve the problem at hand.

Asking yourself "What else?" is pushing your brain just a little further than you're currently pushing it. It's forcing yourself to think beyond the obvious. It's asking yourself to question what you know and test your assumptions. Have you really tried everything?

"What Else?" Works

In the late 1990s, Procter & Gamble set out to make a better soap for cleaning floors. P&G was already a world leader in consumer products for the home, but they realized that mopping was a problematic chore that people hated. Mopping involved filling a bucket full of water and soap, hauling the heavy bucket around the house, risking sloshing water everywhere, wringing the mop over and over, and near the end of the chore looking down at the dirty bucket of mop water and realizing that there was more dirt than soap in the bucket. There was room for improvement in the mopping process, to say the least.

P&G thought that better, more efficient soap might make the cleaning process go more smoothly. They wondered if they could create a soap that would cut through grime in the mop bucket and keep the water cleaner throughout the entire mopping process. Armed with that goal, the P&G research team went to visit homes and watch people mop their floors.

At each home, the P&G observers asked the study participants to mop the floors while they watched and took notes on the process. As they struggled through the cumbersome process, most individuals followed the same steps of getting the mop head wet with soap and water, running the mop along the floors, and then rinsing out the mop head in the bucket of soap and water. After the observations had been completed, P&G researchers replayed hours of video footage of people mopping their floors and realized something: Half of the time, the moppers weren't actually mopping. They were cleaning the mop. Cleaning off the mop in the bucket of soap and water or getting a fresh bucket of soap and water when the first bucket got dirty…that process took at least as much time as actually cleaning the floor.

P&G had started with a question: "How can we make strong soap for floors?" Soon they realized that was the wrong question. When they asked themselves, "*What else* besides soap makes the process of mopping so onerous?" they started to see a new answer emerge. P&G's team realized that the key to fixing mopping wasn't a stronger soap. It was a new mop—a mop that cleaned yet didn't need to BE cleaned.

The team got to work, and the iconic Swiffer product was born. It provided a bucket-free, dirty-water-free mopping experience that solved the problems consumers were experiencing. But Swiffer never would have existed if the P&G team hadn't asked themselves, "What else could we do to solve this problem besides what we assumed?"

Instead of thinking, "It is what it is,"
ask yourself, "What else?"

Think of how often we accept a situation at face value. "It is what it is" has become a popular phrase to describe dismissing a situation as unchangeable and unfixable. But if we were to ask, "What else could it be?" or "What else could be possible?" we might find that the situation isn't as rigid as it might appear.

Try an experiment: for a single day, ask yourself "What else?" as many times as possible.

- What else could my boss be looking for in this report before I hand it in?

- What else could my sister have meant when she made that statement that hurt my feelings?

- What else could be going on in my friend's life that caused her to forget to call?

- What else could really impress the client?

- What else could I say or do to make my partner's day?

See how many ways "what else" can be used? Answering that question can soothe hurt feelings, inspire higher-quality work, and build stronger relationships. Instead of thinking, "It is what it is," ask yourself, "What else?" Asking "what else" is a powerful strategy for digging deeper into any situation and coming up with fresh answers.

Analysis Paralysis

There's a question that often comes up in some form in the process of generating as many ideas and options as possible: *How many is too many?* Can you ask yourself, "What else?" too many times? Is it possible to generate so many options that you freeze up at the number of choices?

This concept of feeling overwhelmed by too many choices is called "analysis paralysis," and for many people it's a real concern. People who experience analysis paralysis often describe not wanting to make choices because they fear making a wrong choice. Instead of making a decision or testing their choices, these individuals tend to get trapped in a long cycle of overanalyzing—a cycle that prevents them from moving forward.

A woman came up to me after one of my presentations and asked, "If I generate too many choices, I'll have analysis paralysis. I can't keep asking myself, 'What else?' or else all those options are going to be too much for me. What should I do?"

I expressed to her that it must be difficult to feel so overwhelmed by choices. "Tell me, how many outfits do you have in your closet?" I asked her. "More than 12?"

"Oh yes, tons!" she giggled.

"And the outfit you picked today looks great!" I acknowledged in response. "And did you eat breakfast today?"

"I did," she replied. "I had scrambled eggs with avocado and swiss."

"Good choice," I affirmed. "That sounds delicious. So…that's two decisions you made today out of LOTS of choices available to you. It feels to me like you CAN choose."

"I guess I do decide on some things. But not the important things," she admitted.

"Ah! I think that's the catch!" I said. "Analysis paralysis doesn't happen because you have too many *choices*. It happens because you have too much *doubt*—doubt in your decision-making abilities, doubt about how good your choices are. You're mixing up the problem. You're making it about your inability to choose between too many options. But the number of options isn't the problem. If you figured out *why* you're doubting yourself and your choices, you wouldn't feel paralyzed anymore."

That audience member helped me articulate analysis paralysis in a way I'd never thought of it before. She could make decisions—just not ones that she perceived as important. She had an idea of herself as a person who couldn't be trusted to make big choices. But if not her, then who?

For her, as with many others, analysis paralysis was never about having too many options. It was about harboring too much doubt.

If you're a person who deals with analysis paralysis or sometimes hesitates with decision-making, don't use that as a reason to run away from thinking up options and making choices. Use it as a catalyst to practice. Start by appreciating the small decisions you make all the time (like picking out an outfit or choosing what to eat), then begin making increasingly larger decisions. Remind yourself of the following truths about decisions:

- No one is in a better position to make choices about your life than you. If not you, then who?

- There's very little that cannot be undone. It may take effort, but most decisions can be reversed.

- Failing to make a decision can have equally (or more!) real and damaging consequences than making the "wrong decision." Not making a choice doesn't protect you—it only forces you into a set of outcomes you didn't choose.

- In ambiguous situations, every problem has more than one right answer.[3] This isn't a math test. You're not searching for the single right choice; you're searching for a path forward that makes sense.

- If your goal is to make a good choice, having more options is the best strategy to accomplish that. Having fewer options may seem like an easier decision, but you could be missing out on a smart alternative.

Choices and Control

In business and in life, having more choices does more than just help you make a smart tactical decision. It also provides a mental reward you might not have expected.

When you're facing change and uncertainty, it's common to feel powerless. Prior to the change, you probably set everything up in your life to go smoothly. You may have had a process for getting through your work and your personal life that made sense, and you had lined things up in a way to make sure you could be as successful as possible. But then change happened, and everything flipped upside down. You're forced to alter your processes. You're forced to shift your goals. Things aren't running smoothly on autopilot anymore. The power you had before—the power to control how things turned out—is gone.

"Self-efficacy" is the term for how much power and control you feel you have over your own circumstances. If you feel you have the skills, talents, and resources to be successful in your current environment, you probably feel high self-efficacy. But when you feel like you don't have what it takes to thrive, you're experiencing low self-efficacy.

When you generate a list of possibilities for moving forward, your self-efficacy naturally starts to increase. You start to realize you do have power, because you have an entire slate of choices from which to pick. You *do* have options. You *do* have control. Your confidence starts to return as your sense of self-efficacy grows.

The Goldilocks Paradox is a trap. Three or fewer options isn't enough to make smart decisions in critical times. Coming up with four or more options serves you both externally and internally. Externally, you'll make better decisions because quantity equals quality. Internally, you'll feel your personal power and confidence increase.

When change forces you to reconsider your path, don't limit yourself by considering only a handful of options. Keep generating ideas until you are confident you have exhausted the possibilities—and then push through the creativity block to generate some more. You'll be amazed at the new paths that open to you.

Chapter 7

Lightening Up

"Without leaps of imagination or dreaming, we lose
the excitement of possibilities. Dreaming, after all,
is a form of planning."—Gloria Steinem

*I*f it feels difficult to get creative, it's not your fault. We live in a society that values concrete contributions and quantifiable success. By the time we're out of elementary school, we're applauded for being able to find the "right" answer fast and getting our work done without fuss. And in adulthood, the opportunities for creative work can feel limited.

But that's what problem-solving is: creative work. We should be doing it every day.

The issue is our vocabulary. For too long, we've talked about creativity as being solely the job of artists, actors, and writers. The rest of us who don't work in entertainment fields aren't "creative types." And those "creative types" have been stereotyped as being emotional, flighty, or not very dependable.[1] Because we've created this line in the sand—a distinction between "us" and "them"—sometimes it can feel hard to become a "creative type" when we really need to. And we all need to. No one is exempt from the job of having to come up with creative solutions to the problems we face at work and at home.

Your challenge, then, is to find ways to lighten up. When you experience levity, fun, and humor, you're more likely to open up your thought process to new ideas. You're more likely to make connections you might not have made. And you're more likely to generate the options you need to move forward.

The Rise of the Fun Workplace

The idea that happy people make better employees isn't a new concept. It's the motivation behind the current increase of workplace culture awards—employers know that employees want to enjoy their jobs. Eighty-one percent of employees who work for an organization on Fortune's "100 Best Companies to Work For" list say their workplace is a "fun" place to work.[2]

Allowing lightheartedness in the workplace provides more than just a feel-good benefit. It also produces better results—and there's a biological reason for this. One of the molecules used in learning and memory is called BDNF, brain-derived neurotropic factor. The more BDNF in your system, the higher your neuroplasticity and ability to form new pathways in the brain. How do you increase BDNF in your system? Play and exercise seem to be the two most consistent ways to enhance BDNF production. The sillier and more physical you get, the bigger the BDNF boost.[3]

A sense of levity makes for a better workplace *and* a better work product. Organizations that nurture creative activity have lower turnover, less absenteeism, faster project completion times, increased teamwork, higher job satisfaction, and higher customer satisfaction.[4] By every measure, adding fun and creativity to your work isn't a distraction; it's a benefit.

A sense of levity makes for a better
workplace and a better work product.

Joanie couldn't wait to start her new job. She was counting down the last two weeks of work at her old office, where her boss treated everyone like they were lazy grifters slacking off on company time. She had enjoyed the work at first, but after the first six months she realized the company culture was built on distrust and demands. When she met her goals, nobody noticed. When she took on extra work, nobody thanked her. The only time anybody seemed to pay attention to Joanie or her colleagues was when a mistake occurred. Joanie missed that feeling of being a valued contributor. After four years, Joanie was ready to move on.

"I'll keep my head down and do a good job," Joanie thought as she walked into her new office on the first day. "Then nobody will have anything to complain about."

She was welcomed to her new office by her boss and direct teammates. They held out a coffee mug with the company logo on it. "First things first," Sarah, her new boss, said. "Let's show you where the break room is. Do you drink coffee? We didn't make you any yet because we don't know how you take it."

The rest of the day the team had booked Joanie for a robust onboarding session. She met with each member of her new team individually for 15 minutes. She was taken around and introduced to other key staff with whom she would work directly. Finally, they brought her into the conference room so the team could meet as a whole and get her up to speed on their current projects.

As Joanie took her seat in the conference room, she looked up at the wall opposite the door. The wall was covered in a giant dry erase board, with "Wall of Wisdom" written across the top. How had she not noticed the board before? All across the wall, in different colors and different handwriting, were dated phrases. None of them made any sense to Joanie.

"This has nothing to do with Victor's bananas. 4/18/19"

"Watch out! The toner tray is big mad today. 11/2/2017"

Joanie gestured to the board. "What's the Wall of Wisdom?" she asked her new boss. Sarah explained that the wall was a running list of funny things that had been said around the office. Over the years, employees would add to this list any time someone said something amusing (especially if the phrase sounded even funnier out of context!). Several of the sayings had become inside jokes and little mantras that the team would repeat regularly during the work week.

Joanie realized she couldn't wait to be a part of this team—it was the only way she would learn about Victor's bananas. She smiled as she pulled out her notebook and pen and prepared to take notes at the meeting. As Sarah and her new colleagues caught her up, Joanie found herself nodding. But she stopped nodding when she realized that Sarah had asked her a question.

"So what do you think we should do about the proposal?" Sarah probed.

"What?" Joanie perked up. "Are you asking me? I don't know—I mean, I'm just getting the background. I don't know enough yet to know what you should do."

"What *we* should do," Sarah responded. "And that's why I'm asking. You don't have any preconceived ideas about the project, so I'd like your take on it. The first two things we've tried haven't been home runs. So I want your eyes on it. Plus, I want you to feel some ownership of the proposal. People support what they help build. So c'mon, help us build this."

Joanie closed her eyes. She hadn't been asked to contribute at work in a long time. But she wanted to impress Sarah, so she thought back to some suggestions she had wanted to make at her old job but knew she couldn't. She and her team played with the ideas for about 45 minutes, and then it was the end of Joanie's first day. Joanie felt like she'd contributed more in a single day than she had in four years at her old job. And she felt smart, like she'd tapped into a well of knowledge she hadn't used in years.

When Joanie arrived home from her first day of work, she told her wife all about her successes. She told her about the introductions, the Wall of Wisdom, and how she was asked to give ideas in the team meeting. Joanie could barely contain her excitement over how fun it all felt. They got a ton of work done, but it was enjoyable. After 15 minutes, Joanie's wife switched gears. She reminded her that they needed to talk with the kids about the chore chart, especially now that Joanie might be working longer hours.

"I have an idea," Joanie said. "I thought about it today in my last meeting. Instead of you and I making up a chore chart for the kids, let's get them involved. People support what they help build, you know? And we can make it a game—instead of us telling them what their chores are for the week, what if we put all the chores in a bowl and each draw chores? We can do it on Sunday afternoons. That way they'll feel like they get a say in it, and there will be an added element of fun."

"I like it," her wife responded. "If they drew their chores out of the bowl instead of us assigning them, then they'll feel more responsible for actually doing them. Smart game!"

Joanie smiled and nodded. It was like her brain was actually working differently today, and it felt good.

Don't buy into the myth that you have to suffer, struggle, and be serious in order to be excellent. In both your work and your life, having fun increases the chances that you'll be able to tap into creative problem-solving energy when you need it.

Finding Your Flow

Creative play is a useful tool because it allows you to be creative without having to be a "creative type" person. It doesn't matter what your profession is—anyone can play! Many forms of creative play invite you to practice on-the-spot problem solving. For example, improvisational theater ("improv" for short) is an activity widely regarded for its ability to help people break out of their routine and generate more original ideas on their feet.[5] Improv is an unscripted, spontaneous type of performance. Participants make up the "scene" on the spot, often guided by cues from the audience or fellow participants.

In improv, the skill of being able to go with the flow is paramount. And that skill can translate from the stage into real life. Dr. Beth Hagenlocker is one of the founders of The Detroit Creativity Project. She and her husband, actor Marc Evan Jackson, were settled in Los Angeles when they connected with a group of other Detroit-raised entertainers in L.A. These Detroit transplants wanted to give back to the hometown that had given them so much, so they started thinking of ways they could contribute to help children. Sixty percent of Detroit children live in poverty, and 25 percent won't graduate from high school.

Jackson had kept ties with a strong network of fellow performers from Detroit Second City. He and his colleagues each had backgrounds in different types of improvisational performance, and they hoped that improv could make a difference in these kids' lives, just as it had in theirs. Improv, the group knew, taught you about more than just being funny.

"Improv helps you be more flexible," Hagenlocker says. "With improv, you learn the value of listening to what other people say before you respond. It's life skills, not just stage skills."

Life skills were exactly what these at-risk teenagers needed, the group realized. They reached out to schools and started promoting a low-cost, low-overhead afternoon improv program for children. This free-to-the-kids program brings teaching artists right into the schools and serves over 1,000 children every year.

Why Improv Makes You More Resilient, According to The Detroit Creativity Project

- Improv teaches the benefits of sticking with something to the end. In The Detroit Creativity Project, at-risk students learn not to give up in the middle of a scene, even if it's messy. Instead of avoiding doing something because you don't know what the outcome is going to be, you can build the confidence to make it through the mess to the other side.

- In improv, it's okay not to have all the answers, and it's okay to make mistakes. Mistakes are just an experiment.

- Improv gives you the power of knowing that your ideas are going to be heard and accepted. The #1 tenet of improv is saying "yes." You don't always have to agree with what someone says, but you have to make space for their viewpoint and build from there.

- We are all already improvisors. We're improvising our lives every day. By practicing improv, you acknowledge that life is unpredictable, and you're committed to getting better at responding.

- Improv is about group storytelling. You don't have to do it alone, and in fact you shouldn't do it alone, because the work gets better when you do it in conjunction with others.

Hagenlocker explains that in improv, you learn how to adapt and respond when you're in an uncertain situation. Or as one of The Detroit Creativity Project students says, "Improv is a way to roll with the punches." You don't know exactly what's going to happen, but the point is to think on your feet and come up with an answer. "When the children get regular practice dealing with the unexpected without losing their cool," Hagenlocker says, "they gain confidence, realizing that they can manage what comes their way in real life."

The Detroit Creativity Project became a success, with teachers reporting that attendance was improving and students were participating more in class and making academic progress. The University of Michigan wanted to find out more about why improv seemed to lead to success for these students. They conducted a three-year study and discovered that kids in The Detroit Creativity Project program had gained confidence, increased their social skills, and reduced their social anxiety, which translated into academic and, later, professional success.

For Hagenlocker, the study results weren't surprising: "Improv frees these kids up to look at all the possible options in their life. For example, we play a game called 'new choice.' In 'new choice,' the kids are asked to replay the same event over again, but from a different perspective. For a lot of kids in the community, their view of life is just what's right in front of them. If we can break that open and allow them to see more, their potential would be limitless."

Looking at all the possible options in your life is exactly what creativity is all about. And it doesn't have to be accomplished by sitting at a desk with a pen in your hand, actively willing yourself to come up with more ideas. In fact, you could argue that it CAN'T be accomplished that way. Maybe it can be accomplished only if you're willing to bring some levity and playfulness into your thought process.

Creative play, as with improv, enhances adaptability and resilience and boosts problem-solving and communication skills.

That's what Robert Rasmussen, the architect of the LEGO® SERIOUS PLAY® (LSP) method, thinks. Rasmussen realized that children's LEGO toys could be used to help solve adult problems in the workplace. In developing the LSP method, Rasmussen tapped into people's desire to participate and take action, as well as their desire to have fun. In traditional work meetings, problem-solving can be stifled because participants don't feel the urge to contribute. A lack of partic-ipation means a lack of ideas and a lack of buy-in. With LSP, however, organizations can encourage a fresh perspective in meetings.

Imagine walking into a meeting and instead of stacks of photo-copied reports you see a pile of colorful toys strewn across the tables.

Immediately, you know THIS meeting won't be like the other meetings. Then you're told you can play freely with whatever you want while other people are talking. It's not just okay—it's actively encouraged! You're told to keep your hands busy playing during the reports. No one is concerned that your free play will negatively impact your focus. Instead, the invitation to play is treated as an invitation to think more deeply about what people are discussing in the meeting.

One reason Rasmussen thinks LSP works so well is that participants are using their hands, which allows their mind to be in a less linear state. Building with LEGOs can get your mind wandering, which you learned in chapter 5 is a great way to generate new ideas.

And when it comes time to transition into problem-solving mode, organizations using LSP are encouraged to build their answers out of LEGOs rather than just state them in words. With building, the entire team participates, not just the small fraction who may speak up in typical meetings. Companies like IKEA, Samsung, and Virgin Atlantic have all used LSP in meetings, and employees confirm that it helps them generate novel ideas they never would have conceived without the added creativity brought on by playing.

Playing Around

What could "play" look like in your world? How could you invite some lightheartedness into your day-to-day life or work? If you have young children, it would be easy to engage in a game of make-believe with them that would delight them and help you let loose. One of my most memorable hours babysitting a friend's son was when we got caught up in a game of "would a ghost be able to do that?" We spent over 90 minutes debating whether or not a ghost even HAD teeth, let alone whether or not he'd be able to brush them. Can a ghost sit in a car seat? Can a ghost eat a milkshake? The world may never know.

Game 1: The Props Game

Even if you don't have small children around, you can spend time being more playful. One of my favorite ways to get my creative juices flowing is based on an improv activity called "the props game." I saw it for the first time on the television show *Whose Line Is It Anyway?* In the props game, four improv actors take the stage in two teams of two. Each team is given a strange set of props. The props are usually oversized and unrecognizable—nothing you'd have lying around the house or had ever seen before. The goal is for each pair to come up with as many uses for their props as they can before time runs out. When the buzzer sounds, the team that has come up with the most potential uses for their props wins.

To play the props game at home, all you need is a household object. Try to grab something you don't use every day—maybe pull something out of the toolbox or the junk drawer in the kitchen. Try to think up alternate uses for this object: What else could it be besides what it actually is? Remember, asking "what else?" over and over helps us dig deeper to get beyond the obvious answers. Could a pair of pliers also be a dental tool? Could it be a replacement for Captain Hook's hand if he lost his hook? Could it be a pair of tweezers for a giant? Could it be a hedge trimmer for very tiny trees in front of a dollhouse?

Your responses don't have to be brilliant. You just have to be willing to be silly and let the ideas flow. The point is that you're practicing to be prepared for those moments that ARE important, when you need to generate ideas in a pinch.

Game 2: The Emotions Game

Here's another improv-type exercise you can use to flex your creativity muscle: Write down a list of eight to ten emotions. You might include things like anger, confusion, sadness, joy, and surprise.

Once you have your list of emotions, think about a sentence you say on a regular basis. It can be a sentence you use in your work life or your home life, but it should be something you say out loud. Maybe "What's for dinner?" or "There's a meeting in the conference room."

Now, look at the first emotion on the list. Repeat the sentence you just wrote in the style of that emotion. So if the first emotion is anger, how would you say, "There's a meeting in the conference room" in an angry way? Maybe the meeting in the conference room isn't supposed to be there, and now you'll look disorganized in front of your client because you have to find a new location for your meeting.

Go down the list and repeat the same sentence, each time in the style of the various emotions. You'll see as you go along that there are so many ways to say the exact same phrase, but it can have a different meaning depending on the emotion you bring to it. In other words, there are a hundred different ways to do anything we do. There isn't one single "right answer" or "right path."

In today's world, it can be hard to let your creative juices flow. But if you allow space in your life for lightness and fun, you'll be much more likely to find creative solutions when you need them.

What Are My Options?

It's time to pause and make a list of options for your new path forward. Remember, the goal doesn't necessarily need to change—only the plan to get there.

Use the strategies you've learned thus far to brainstorm as many possibilities as you can. Avoid the Goldilocks Paradox: don't limit yourself to only three options. Engage in creative problem-solving to generate options that push you past your gut instinct—options that might even make you uncomfortable. Don't worry about how practical or effective the plans seem at this point. In the next part of this book, you'll learn techniques for narrowing down your options to pinpoint the path that is right for you.

PART 3

MOVE ON

Chapter 8

The Art of Deciding

"The secret of change is to focus all of your energy
not on fighting the old, but on building the new."
—Socrates

*n*ow that you've generated several options for your revised plan, it's time to move forward. This final stage of the three stages, Move On, is when you'll focus on turning your ideas into action. At this stage the question becomes: *Which option do you choose? How do you know which one to pick and where to go from here?*

When I was in high school, I worked as a lifeguard during the summers. Lifeguard training was one of the most difficult challenges of my life up until that point. To be a lifeguard, you have to be certified in CPR, first aid, and pass several fitness tests both in and out of the water. I had to tread water for several minutes with a ten-pound brick over my head, not letting the brick touch the water. I had to perform a deep-water rescue on my instructor (who was the burly high school football coach) as he thrashed around and pretended to be aggressively resisting my attempts to save him. I was a 14-year-old non-athlete, but I beat everyone's expectations and passed the lifeguard exam.

That first summer, the most exciting thing that happened was learning how to twirl a whistle. But the second summer I learned why my instructor had been so serious about our skills. In the second summer, there was an incident.

It happened quietly, like pool accidents often do. Too quietly, in fact. Our community pool was laid out with three lifeguard chairs: one over the shallow end, one over the middle, and one over the deep end near the diving boards. There were always four lifeguards on duty, rotating stations every 15 minutes. You'd sit by the shallow end area, then the middle, then the deep end, then go on break, repeating the same pattern every hour.

But the changeover every 15 minutes is the trickiest time. You see, lifeguards aren't allowed to just turn their back on the pool and climb out of their chair. Someone has to be scanning the pool at all times. The rotation goes like this: the lifeguard coming back from break walks out at the appointed time. They stand next to the shallow end chair and begin to scan the pool. While the new lifeguard is scanning beside them, the lifeguard in the shallow end chair gets out of the chair and climbs down. That lifeguard then takes back over scanning the shallow end area while the lifeguard coming back from break climbs up into the chair. When the new lifeguard is in the shallow end chair, the lifeguard who had previously been in the shallow end chair walks over to the middle chair and watches the pool while the process of climbing in and out of the lifeguard chair repeats. At all times, someone is scanning the pool in every area.

One July afternoon, I was waiting impatiently for changeover time. I was sitting in the middle chair, and I was about to be relieved to move over into the deep end chair for 15 minutes, and then it would be my break time. When my coworker came to relieve me and I climbed out of the middle chair, I started scanning the pool while he climbed up. Everything looked fine. Everything was quiet.

But something was still wrong—not in the pool, but around it. I noticed the lifeguard chair over the deep end was empty. My coworker,

Molly, wasn't in the chair. I raced over to the deep end and found Molly in the diving well with two children. A young boy had gotten impatient and jumped off the diving board too soon, landing on top of a small girl. Molly had seen it happen and jumped in without first blowing her whistle. In her panic, she had forgotten to alert the rest of us.

In that moment, I learned why lifeguards always have to be scanning the pool at every changeover: we have to know the lay of the land before we move forward. If we don't take a good hard look at what's going on around us, we don't know how to make the right decision. There won't always be a whistle or a big red flag to alert us. It's up to us to look for ourselves, gather information, and know our surroundings before we act. Luckily, Molly had reacted quickly and was able to keep both children safe. But if I hadn't been scanning, I would have missed the whole thing.

At this stage, you're being challenged to select the best path forward from all your options. Your job, much like a lifeguard's job, is to look at your surroundings, understand the threats and opportunities, and then take action. It's time now to take a hard look at the options you've generated in previous chapters and choose a course of action so you can move forward successfully.

Reject the Obvious

Knowing which ideas are worth pursuing is a unique type of intellectual ability.[1] Selecting how to move forward will require you to weigh pros and cons, imagine the potential future outcomes of each choice, and think about whom and what your decisions will impact.

As you look through your options, some paths will be easy to eliminate. You can begin narrowing down your options by considering whether some of them just don't make sense. Imagine you're a weight-lifter who has been invited to compete in the next Olympics. Your goal is to be able to lift 827 pounds (about 375 kg) by the day of your Olympic competition. You and your coach make a training plan, and you begin by listing out all the programs you may want to follow. Should you really consider the option where you show up the day before the Olympics, load 827 pounds on a bar, and commit to staying there until you can make that bar budge? Of course not. You can cross that one right off the list.

The right training program is probably some version of "lift as much as you can today. Then increase the weight gradually between now and the Olympics until you can lift 827 pounds." How many pounds you should add at a time and how quickly you should increase those increments…well, those are the different elements of the successful plan. There are likely several different training regimens that would work. But "just try really hard the night before" is clearly not the right plan.

It's good to have lots of options, as we discussed in the previous chapters. But it's also okay to cross some of them off the list once you come to this stage. When the wrong move is clear, the right moves become more apparent.

When the wrong move is clear, the right
moves become more apparent.

Scrutinize the Shortcuts

Once you've narrowed down your list by removing the obvious, take a hard look at what's left. A frontrunner often starts to emerge at this stage—a plan that seems like it will be the fastest path to success. That may feel good, but don't celebrate just yet. The frontrunner could be a trap.

Most people are familiar with the story of Rosa Parks: how she was tired from cleaning houses all day but the bus was full, so she sat down in the only empty spot and refused to give up her seat to a white person and thus inadvertently kicked off the Montgomery bus boycott and became a civil rights hero.

But the story we know about Rosa Parks is wrong. It's completely backwards. In reality, Rosa Parks had already been a leader in the local movement for civil rights. Some of her contemporaries claimed she had been sitting on several buses in the preceding weeks, trying to bring attention to the cause. This one day it finally worked. But it wasn't an accident. Rosa Parks meant to do what she did.

When we tell the story of Rosa Parks as though she was an accidental hero, we're looking for a shortcut. We're looking for a magic wand we can wave and say, "This one pivotal moment just happened, and she became a household name." If you've ever heard a famous person joke, "Oh yeah, it took me 20 years to become an overnight sensation!" they're making fun of society's tendency to glamorize shortcuts and pretend that years of struggle didn't happen just because we didn't see it. Rosa Parks took no shortcuts. She worked and struggled, and she finally got the recognition she deserved for her efforts.

In contemporary times, it's tempting to look at people we admire and want to replicate their success. We think, *I want what they have. If I could just reverse engineer so-and-so's path, that'll be exactly where I want to go.* In truth, it's nearly impossible to reverse engineer someone else's success. Like with Rosa Parks, we often don't hear the real story. We hear an overly simplistic version, or we witness one strategy or effort and assume it is responsible for their achievement.

We take this reductive narrative and try to map our path to success onto it. The best choice on our list of options becomes the one that seems popular or efficient, but the truth is, we favor this frontrunner only because of emotion and misinformation.

Even if you get advice directly from someone you admire, you can't be sure that it's the *whole* story. Shortly after I started my speaking business, I went to coffee with a guy named Jake. Jake was very generous in offering to give me advice on how to build my business and share secrets he had learned along the way. One of my first questions for Jake was "How did you get your clients?"

Jake proudly responded, "Oh, all my clients come from repeat business and referrals."

"Oh wow, that's great," I replied. "But how did you get your FIRST clients?"

"That's it," he answered. "It's all repeat business and referrals. That's the most efficient way to get clients—if they've already worked with you or someone has seen you."

"Sure, sure, sure," I muttered, trying to figure out a way to make myself clearer. "But what I'm asking is…what about when you had NO business, so there was no business to repeat and no one to refer you. What about then?"

Jake pondered for a moment, looking at his coffee mug. "Well…I don't know…I think I just called people who were already in my database."

Jake wasn't trying to be difficult. He had fallen victim to a phenomenon called "the peak-end effect" (not the weekend effect—that's when you can't remember what happened because you went to the bar with your friends). The peak-end effect is a bias event that happens when your brain is too full of information so it's forced to condense other things to save space. Essentially, your memory reduces large chunks of information so that you retain only the highs, the lows, and the last or most recent occurrence—the peaks and the ends. Everything else becomes a blur. If you can remember the day someone exploded a beaker of foam in science class but not the day before or after, that's the peak-end effect at work.

Thanks to the peak-end effect, we're not very good at remembering the long, slow climb before the peak. We don't tend to retain all the little details of the effort we put in to build toward our first success. So even if you ask someone for advice and they're willing to help, their brain may be preventing them from giving you the true story. They're not glossing over the hard work to trick you; they literally don't remember.

If there's an option on your list that seems like the fastest route to the success you're hoping for, be suspicious. What may look like a shortcut is often just a lack of information. If you're really hoping to construct a life you're proud of, you can't copy someone else's life. You can't cheat by speeding through a trail you think someone else has already blazed. Someone else's footsteps likely aren't going to take you where you need to go, so don't follow them. Instead, recognize that other people's stories have similar struggles to yours, even if they aren't readily visible.

Test the Options

When companies are considering a change in their offerings or entrepreneurs are launching a new idea, they often use a model called "minimum viable product." Like beta testing, with a minimum viable product, leaders create a smaller-scale experience to test. The minimum viable product allows them to dip their toe in the water and get feedback on how their idea might be perceived in the marketplace. They can gather information before they spend significant amounts of time, money, and energy launching the full concept.

Choosing your next path forward shouldn't feel like a game of roulette. You don't have to choose without any information. You can test your options before you fully commit to a single plan. And if you think there's no way to test your options before diving in, consider Calvin's story.

Calvin worked as a manager for an IT services company. The pay was great, and the hours were decent. But after several years, Calvin was starting to get bored. In his role, he didn't get to do as much interfacing with the public as he had hoped, and he felt like he was stagnating. The highlight of his week was spending time doing his volunteer work as a Court Appointed Special Advocate (CASA). CASAs are community volunteers who represent children in court cases involving abuse and neglect. Their role is intended to provide a mouthpiece for the child by interviewing the child and other family members, reviewing documents, attending court, and making sure the child's best interests are represented.

As a CASA, Calvin was advocating for a five-year-old little girl named Aniyah. He had been Aniyah's volunteer for the past 16 months, and he felt like her case was finally coming to a good resolution. His volunteer manager asked him if he wanted to be matched with another child after Aniyah's case was finished. Calvin replied, "I mean, I hadn't thought about it. But of course! Yes, definitely!"

At home that night, Calvin thought about wrapping up Aniyah's case and learning about the next child he was going to help. It was so rewarding, thinking about Aniyah finally being done with court, stable, and ready to move on with her life. *I wish I didn't have to do this only on evenings and weekends*, Calvin thought to himself. In that moment, Calvin startled himself. *Why DO I do this only on evenings and weekends?* he thought. *Why couldn't I do this full time if I wanted?* Calvin hopped out of bed and started researching the requirements for getting into law school. He was old for law school, but it was possible. He could get a law degree and become a lawyer, helping kids like Aniyah full time.

Calvin didn't realize it, but he was testing his options. By volunteering, he was trying his hand at an interest without having to take the risk of quitting his full-time job before he knew if he liked it or was good at it. Volunteering is an ideal way of testing options, and it can be done in many fields. Want to be an event planner? Volunteer to help a nonprofit plan a fundraising gala. Interested in technology? Many nonprofit programs need help building up-to-date technology. Thinking about a career in government? Sit on a community committee and watch government in action.

In both your personal life and professional life, there are usually creative ways to take your ideas for a test drive before you commit. Just like you wouldn't marry someone on a first date, it's good to gather information about a potential new plan at the beginning.

How Do You Measure Success?

When it comes to considering your options, it helps to know what end result you're aiming for. You can't plan to be successful until you know how success is measured. What will success look like for you? Is it happiness? Recognition? A sense of security?

Colonel Randall Larsen, USAF (retired), was the executive director of the Congressional Commission on the Prevention of Weapons of Mass Destruction Proliferation and Terrorism (commonly known as the WMD Commission) in 2009 and 2010. The Commission was a bipartisan project under then-President Barack Obama, aimed at protecting the United States from terrorist threats.

Launched in March of 2009, the Commission would encounter one of its first "aha!" moments relatively quickly: on April 15th of that same year, the H1N1 swine flu was first detected in a human in California. Within a week, more infections were reported across the country, and within two weeks the government had declared swine flu a public health emergency.

The realization of the Commission had significant implications: the United States was potentially more vulnerable to a biological attack than the nuclear attack we had long been fearing. To protect ourselves, we would need to be prepared for biological warfare. The Commission began researching potential responses to bioterrorism. Viral vaccines were at the forefront of their minds, given that the H1N1 pandemic was still a global threat. As they researched, a scary pattern emerged: there weren't enough vaccines to go around.

Colonel Larsen recalls, "The chief scientist on our project was seven-and-a-half months pregnant. She was in the most at-risk category, and even SHE couldn't get a vaccine. That's how severe the vaccine shortage was. We realized right there that THAT was the story. The entire world was at risk from bioterrorism. We wouldn't be able to protect ourselves against a virus."

In 2009, vaccines were still created using chicken eggs. It was a cost-effective, if slow, process. There was little financial incentive, Larsen explains, to do it any differently. But if we were going to protect ourselves from bioterrorism, the Commission reported, we were going to need to speed up the vaccine production process.

The Commission's early focus had been on gathering information. But now they had an even more critical, time-sensitive task ahead of them. Their focus went from "How do we gather this information?" to "How do we get this information out to the public? How do we get people to actually pay attention to this?"

As Colonel Larsen considered his options, he knew it could be foolish to hope that the report would naturally get attention. There was a running inside joke that congressional commissions put out reports that became "shelfware," meaning they collected dust on a shelf somewhere. He could consider reaching out to the traditional press, but that might earn a day's worth of coverage and then disappear.

Colonel Larsen realized his best bet was to throw out the traditional playbook and try something that had never been done before. He and his team created Facebook, Twitter, and YouTube accounts. They produced and created a short video documentary titled *Faster Vaccines*, aimed at helping average citizens understand the public benefit that could be gained by being able to produce vaccines with a quicker turnaround time. Within a few weeks, President Obama had seen the video and committed to making updating vaccine technology a priority. The bipartisan WMD Commission agreed.

In his role, Colonel Larsen challenged "the way we've always done it" in several ways. First, the project called out decades of stagnation in vaccine innovation and production. Some of the groundwork laid in speeding up vaccine production since that time can be credited with the ability to quickly produce vaccines against the novel coronavirus in the COVID-19 pandemic. Second, Colonel Larsen refused to simply release a report the way commissions "always do it." Instead, he engaged US citizens and used public interest to get leaders to pay attention to the story.

Colonel Larsen defined success by how much change he could effect quickly, and that definition influenced all his choices. His goal was to protect people, and his decisions were a matter of life and death. The stakes couldn't have been higher. His choice to leverage social media was unusual and risky, but it paid off.

As you move forward, know what success looks like for you. The clearer you can be about what's flexible and what's non-negotiable, the more straightforward your decisions will become. Decision-making is never easy, but once you put parameters in place, you'll find it less intimidating. In the next two chapters, we're going to explore even more strategies you can use to weigh your options and make a choice.

Chapter 9

Stories Solve Problems

"The intelligent have plans; the wise have principles."—Raheel Farooq

*E*xperiences help us make smart decisions. Every life event and challenge you face earns you wisdom that can help you move forward in the future. But each of us has only so many life experiences from which we can draw. There will always be unfamiliar situations that come up and brand-new territories to navigate. How are you supposed to make a smart decision if you've never experienced a particular set of circumstances before?

The secret lies in multiplying your knowledge. You can't know what you don't know. But you *can* know what *other* people know. All you have to do is ask.

Humans have the ability to learn from the stories that other people tell. If you listen, you can grow from their experience without having to live through the experience yourself. In the previous chapter, we covered how knowing a little bit about other people's stories doesn't mean you can simply reverse engineer their success. But hearing stories from other people can still benefit you, especially if you collect stories from multiple people, with multiple points of view. The key is to gather information with the intention to problem-solve, rather than trying to take a shortcut.

By paying attention to the stories other people tell, you're keeping a running inventory of what works and what doesn't. You're gathering information about situations you've never faced before so you'll be ready to face them in the future. To tap into the wisdom of others, listen to their stories.

But there's a problem. People often avoid stories. Organizations, especially, seem to avoid stories. At work, decision-making is often based solely on strategic plans and checklists and flowcharts. Stories don't appear to fit into the accepted culture of how decisions are reached. Stories can seem too touchy-feely. But the United States Military doesn't agree. The US Military recognizes the power in using stories to guide decision-making.

Several years ago, the US Military became interested in teaching adaptability to their troops. Until that time, most soldier recruits had been trained using a technique called "errorless training." The basis of errorless training is skills drilling. You perform a skill over and over again until you don't make any mistakes. When you can repeat the skill without error, you're considered to have mastered the skill. Errorless training made up a large segment of the training received by military recruits.

But then the military launched an experiment. They took a group of new recruits and split them into two teams. The first team received the traditional program of errorless training. But the second team got something innovative. Not only did they receive the same errorless training as the first team, but they also received something called "error exposure training." In error exposure training, the soldier recruits were visited by military higher-ups: generals and colonels and other decision-makers. These high-ranking officers detailed their past experiences for the trainees. They talked about battles they had been in, decisions they had made. They shared their thought processes and what had influenced their choices. They talked about what had worked, what didn't—their failures and successes.

After both groups of recruits completed their training, it was time for field testing. The recruits were put into the field in simulations and tested to see how well they could respond to different challenges. The results were clear: the recruits who received error exposure training—who had heard stories from others—made smarter decisions than the recruits trained the old way, with errorless training. The error exposure-trained recruits also made decisions faster than their counterparts. Similar training has been done with other high-stress professions like firefighters and surgeons, and the results confirm the military's experience: error exposure training leads to better, faster decision-making.[1]

When you have not only your own experiences to draw from, but a whole library of experiences, you are able to make smarter decisions when you're in a pinch. Don't make the mistake of viewing stories as too qualitative or overly emotional. If stories aren't too touchy-feely for the military and firefighters, they probably aren't too touchy-feely for you. When you gather stories from other people, you're creating a mental filing cabinet of knowledge that can help you rewrite your plans more successfully than if you tried to do it alone.

This kind of collaborative mindset can make the difference between crafting a new plan that succeeds and creating one that fails. For organizations facing unfamiliar challenges, leaders who gathered and used input from others before making decisions were found to make better choices compared to leaders who made decisions independently. Stakeholder involvement led to decisions that were seen as more effective and were more widely adopted by the group.[2] When you act alone, without hearing the stories of others, you risk making a misstep.

If you want to be successful—even in situations you've never faced before—be willing to draw on others' experience for guidance. Allow them to tell you what they've seen and survived. Pay attention to the choices they made and the outcomes they earned. Their lessons will help you avoid mistakes as you craft your new path.

Tap into the wisdom of others;
listen to their stories.

We Want to Know Why

When listening to the stories of others, it's important to remember that stories don't just tell us WHAT happened. They also help us understand WHY something happened. People need to know WHY. They need context. Studies show that when we give people context for understanding, we're more likely to get what we want.

In 1977, a Harvard professor named Ellen Langer performed a now-famous study on interpersonal interactions that revolved around making photocopies. Langer sent her research assistants into the library when the copy machine had a really long line to see if they could cut the line ahead of other people. First, her research assistant went up to somebody in the long line and said, "Excuse me. I have five pages. May I use the Xerox machine?" About 60 percent of people said, "Yes," and allowed the research assistant to cut the line.

In phase two, the research volunteer tried to cut in line again. This time, they said, "Excuse me, I have five pages. May I use the Xerox machine, because I'm in a rush?" This time, over 94 percent of people tested allowed the researcher to cut the line. Just from hearing that additional word "because," people were so much more willing to comply with the request.

But Langer and her team didn't stop there. In phase three, the researchers tried one more experiment. They approached people in line and said, "Excuse me, I have five pages. May I use the Xerox machine, because I have to make copies?" They didn't say, "Because I'm in a hurry." Not, "Because I have a sick kid." Not, "Because my professor is going to fail me." No truly valid reason. Simply, "Because I have to make copies," and it worked. Ninety-three percent of people tested allowed the researcher to cut the line, nearly the same rate as when the reason was "because I'm in a rush." "Because I have to make copies" is a pitiful excuse. Everyone in line for the photocopy machine has to make copies! And yet, just offering some manner of explanation seemed to work well.[3]

When someone explains themselves, we're much more willing to give them what they want. That's the magic of helping people understand why. Think about how you could use that in your life or in your work. With just a simple explanation—not even a long story, just a tiny little sentence—you can get people more on board with what you want.

In a family, stories help younger generations grasp why we do the things we do—why our traditions exist, why we follow certain family rules. At work, stories are how an entire organization can decode why our clients stay with us, why our team culture is the way it is, why our initiatives are successful (or why they're not). Five or ten years down the road, in the middle of the NEXT crisis, no one will likely remember your flowchart. But they will remember your story.

Give the people in your life stories, because stories explain WHY.

The Screwup Story

One of the most compelling types of stories from which we can learn are stories about failure. These "screwup stories" are rich with information about what NOT to do. In chapter 8, you learned that people are more likely to pinpoint the causes of their failures than the causes of their successes, thanks to the peak-end effect.[4] Here's where you can take advantage of the brain's unique ability to remember the details leading up to big mistakes and learn from the people who've made those mistakes before you. When you listen to the screwup stories of others, you're getting important red flags that can help you avoid failure.

I once screwed up, and the only thing that saved me was someone else sharing their screwup story with me. Before I started speaking and writing, I ran a small, local nonprofit called Austin Involved. As I've touched on before, the concept behind Austin Involved was to get young professionals to commit to giving small amounts of time and money every month so that they could build a greater habit of giving and community involvement. As someone who had grown up volunteering and spent time working in the nonprofit field, I was a regular giver. But many of my friends and acquaintances weren't. People would say things to me like "Oh wow, you're always giving back. I'd do that, but I don't have a lot of time." Or "I don't have enough money." Or "I don't even know any nonprofits."

I created Austin Involved around the giving circle model, where you join as a member and agree to have a $25 donation auto-debited from your bank account every month. Each month we had a different focus area: one month it might be homelessness; another it might be cancer awareness; the next it might be literacy. I would film two-minute videos highlighting all the nonprofits in town that worked in that focus area, and our members would then vote for the nonprofit they wanted to win. Every member's $25 donation for the month earned them the right to vote. The nonprofit with the most votes got the whole kitty of everyone's monthly $25 contribution, along with a three-hour service project, where our members volunteered in a hands-on way.

By the end of a year or two of membership in Austin Involved, you would have been able to see dozens of local nonprofits in action. Then you could take your $300 a year (which you might have realized a) was not too hard to donate after all and b) really made an impact in the community) and give it directly to one of the nonprofits you had discovered along the way. We even created a training program to teach our young professionals how to join a nonprofit board of directors and be a contributing board member.

Austin Involved garnered lots of attention. We were featured in the press. I won some awards. Then we were approached to merge with a larger nonprofit in town. This nonprofit had an admirable goal of increasing charitable giving in our area, but they weren't having as much luck reaching younger donors. They knew they needed to attract the 20- and 30-something crowd that was growing in Austin. So they wanted to merge with us and gain our younger members.

My immediate response was to feel flattered. Someone wanted something I had built! It was valuable enough that they were offering to pay me a good salary! I wouldn't have to fundraise every penny I earned anymore! The board of directors of Austin Involved and I made the decision to join forces and merge, hoping we would be stronger together. It meant trading in my yoga pants for actual work clothes and my home office for a downtown view. I was pumped. I felt so proud of myself. But I hadn't considered all the repercussions.

And not too long after the merger, my ego got involved.

In the new organization, I wasn't the boss anymore. I still ran the operations of Austin Involved, but I reported to the leader of the other organization. I didn't get to call the shots anymore. I couldn't fly by the seat of my pants and change up plans because of my instincts—I had to involve three other people and a staff-wide calendar. My tiny little nonprofit was growing, and I was experiencing growing pains.

I started butting heads with my new boss, wondering why processes that had been working for years needed to be updated. I was frustrated at how long decisions were taking with so many staff people involved. I knew, rationally, that the only way for Austin Involved to grow was for there to be more people than just me at the helm. I knew we needed the stability and the staff support that the larger nonprofit provided. But I had become so used to having the final word on everything, and I was having trouble letting go.

After six months, I couldn't take it anymore. I didn't like the short-tempered, stubborn employee I was turning into. I regularly thought about quitting—not because I didn't love Austin Involved or the goal of the new merged organization, but because it was too hard for me not to be the boss anymore.

Sometimes we cling to situations that aren't really serving us because we think we should want them.

One afternoon I had dinner with a friend, Leslie, who also worked in the nonprofit field. She could tell something was bothering me, but I didn't want to admit what was happening. It's embarrassing to talk about your ego, especially as a nonprofit worker. I finally admitted that I was struggling to settle in at the new organization. She somehow knew exactly what I meant.

Leslie explained to me that years ago, she had been serving as the development director in charge of fundraising for a well-known nonprofit. When the executive director left, the board of directors hired Leslie to serve as the interim director while they searched for a new executive director. The search took the better part of the year, and Leslie got used to being the boss. When the new ED was hired, Leslie resumed her original role as the fundraiser. But she struggled with going from *being* the boss to *having* a boss, just like me.

Leslie said, "One day the new ED was praising some of my work at a staff meeting. In my head, I was being snarky, like 'Yeah, no kidding. I'm great at fundraising. And I've been doing my job *and* your job for the past year.' I was thinking snarky thoughts in response to a compliment! And then I realized: Wait, I AM great at my job—the actual job I applied for and was hired to do. *This* is the job that makes me feel fulfilled. I never wanted the ED job; that's not my skillset. I should be happy to go back to the job that suits me best and that I enjoy."

As she was talking, something clicked within me. I'm great at coming up with ideas for programs that solve people's problems. I'm good at getting people excited about those programs and building support for them. But I'm not very good at details. I'm not very good at managing incremental growth. I was suited for the challenges of a startup, but I struggled with the challenges of a mid-sized organization.

I had accepted a job because of the ego boost it provided—not because I would be good at it. Austin Involved had reached a stage in its life cycle where it needed something I couldn't offer. It needed more than me, and I needed to step back and let that happen.

Leslie helped me understand how common it is for people to hang on to roles that don't suit them instead of flourishing in jobs that are meant for them. It happens in our personal lives, too: we can cling to situations that aren't really serving us because we think we *should* want them. But Leslie was right—it was time for me to move on.

There's no need to repeat the mistakes that others have already made and warned you about. Listen to their warnings and learn from their screwup stories.

Gathering Stories

The more stories we have, the more information we can tap into. The more information we can tap into, the more options we can generate. The more options we've generated, the more successful we're likely to be (remember the Goldilocks Paradox from chapter 6!).

Obtaining stories from other people doesn't have to be a formal process. You've already probably gathered stories informally without even realizing it. At work, you know which people are prickly to deal with and must be handled carefully. You know which people are reliable and can always be depended on. You know who likes to chat about non-work topics in the break room. You know this because of your experiences with them, which are stories you've lived through.

Knowing those stories is already helping you to be successful. You know that if it's crunch time and you need help getting a project finished, you want to go to the reliable employee, not the talkative employee. You're using those mental stories already, without realizing it.

If the stories you gathered by accident are serving you, think about how much *more* helpful it would be if you could intentionally tap into stories. That might feel uncomfortable to you—asking for someone to share their story so you can learn from it. But sharing stories is just conversation. You have conversations every day where people share their stories. You may not have been thinking about them as an opportunity to learn, so you may not have been paying close attention to how a given story could apply to you. But if you ask the right questions, you can gather important information to slip into your mental file folder for later use. And as a bonus, people love to talk about themselves! Most people will enjoy sharing their stories, especially if they believe it could help someone they know.

To start getting more comfortable gathering stories from people, you can use these scripted questions to prompt a conversation:

- Why did you make the decision you made?

- What factor was the most important in making that decision?

- What surprised you about that experience you had?

- To whom did you turn for guidance when you were unsure?

- How did you handle any missteps or mistakes?

- What would you do differently if you were to do it again?

- Were you prepared for this challenge? How was it like other situations you've faced before? How was it different?

The questions above aren't just helpful if you're speaking to a mentor or boss. Everyone, regardless of their job title or education, has had experiences you haven't had before. Once you get comfortable asking these questions, you'll find that everyone has a story you can learn from. And when you do, you'll have tapped into an incredible decision-making arsenal that will help you decide how to solve the problem at hand.

Meet the ReVisionary

Amal Safdar Wilemon

From the Runways of NYC to the Studios of Kenya

Two things loomed large in Amal Safdar Wilemon's childhood: her Muslim faith and her love of fashion. Her mother, a Pakistani immigrant to the United States, frequently took Amal and her sisters on shopping trips to Paris and New York City while the girls were growing up. So it was no surprise when, at 19, Amal got a job producing fashion shows for major brands and moved to New York a few years later. She was living her dream. But when she hit her 30s, she realized she wanted more out of life: She wanted to find a partner. She wanted a slower pace. She ducked out of the New York "rat race" and moved back home to Texas.

When Amal met Zane Wilemon shortly after arriving home, it shouldn't have seemed like a perfect match. Zane wasn't just not Muslim—he was an Episcopal priest! Yet on their first date, deep in the middle of a conversation about faith, they realized they both had a deep love for God that seemed more similar than it was different. And Amal felt compelled to help Zane with his work, a two-pronged charitable organization providing health care for special needs children in Kenya and creating work for their mothers. Through the organization Ubuntu Life, these "Maker Moms" create beautiful handmade products like bags, bracelets, and shoes, and earn a living for their families.

Without even meaning to, Amal has found her way back to the world of fashion—but this time inspired by purpose and with her loving husband, Zane, by her side.

Chapter 10

Getting Input = Better Outcomes

"The chameleon changes color to match the earth.
The earth doesn't change color to match
the chameleon."—Senegalese Proverb

*I*f asking other people for their stories and input is such a helpful strategy, why don't we do it more often? When asked that question, the main reason people give for not seeking out information from others is that it feels difficult to ask for help. It can make us feel vulnerable. From a professional angle, some workplace cultures have taught us that if you want to be perceived as competent, you should be able to problem-solve without help. If you expect to rise through the ranks, you should be entirely self-sufficient.

In reality, however, "going it alone" is rarely successful. People who don't ask for help are limited to relying on their own past experiences and their gut instinct when deciding how to move forward. In contrast, people who ask for help get the benefit of multiple points of view, different opinions, and many options for how to continue. Asking others for their input makes sense, yet we often avoid it.

I've been guilty of it, as well. In my first job out of college (at the postcard marketing company), I was given a large project to implement. I had originally been hired to be a salesperson, but the company had acquired a new division the week before my start date.

It made sense to have me handle the background work needed to get the project launched rather than have another employee stop what they were doing mid-project.

The first time I had a problem with the new product launch, I remember thinking, *Oh man. The computer isn't responding to the update. This doesn't make any sense.* After trying and failing several times to make the change I needed to the back end of the program, I turned to my direct boss for help. Russ held up his hand in the gimme-a-minute sign, then turned to me. "What's the problem?"

I explained what was happening, and Russ and I found a solution in about 45 minutes. But two days later, I hit a different roadblock. It was time to start sorting data, but I wasn't clear if Russ and Alan wanted me to sort it by one set of data or another set of data. I could see it working both ways. I didn't want to waste time or bother Russ again by asking for his help, so I did what my mom used to call "making an executive decision." I made the choice I thought was best, and I finished setting up the program to sort data by the values I had selected.

And I was wrong. Leadership took one look and decided it would be better to sort by the other data set. I chose what I thought made sense and moved forward in order to save time. But making the wrong call instead of asking ultimately wasted time.

I realized what I was experiencing is common, particularly in young professionals and early-career employees. We can be conditioned to believe that if we need help, maybe we don't deserve our jobs. It may seem, to a new hire, like everybody else simply *knows* what to do without asking; therefore, we shouldn't need to ask, either. That's the trap I fell into. I thought that if I had to bother people for help, then I might not deserve to have been hired.

I'm not alone. When I surveyed over 1,000 working professionals and asked them about listening to others and getting help when they're dealing with uncertainty, the responses varied widely based on age. The youngest age bracket of employees in the study reported the lowest levels of taking time to understand and embrace solutions presented by their colleagues. More seasoned employees, however, seemed to feel more comfortable gathering ideas from others, possibly because they feel secure in their positions and experience. Despite the reality that early-career employees are likely to have the greatest need for information, context, and guidance to perform their roles effectively, it can be uncomfortable to ask. It can be seen as a sign of weakness.

If we expect to achieve success, that mindset needs to shift. Whatever your age or the length of time you've been in your career, asking for help and input from others needs to become the No. 1 strategy we rely on when we're navigating new waters, instead of a flaw to be avoided.

A Culture of Connection

Goodway Group is an organization that knows good decisions aren't made in a vacuum. As a company, they've faced generations of change. After being founded in 1929 as a printing company, the organization has adapted over the years to stay relevant. Today, they're a digital media company with a 100 percent remote workforce and no in-office employees. The shift to fully remote work happened in 2007, well ahead of the work-from-home trend.

But Goodway knew remote work came with a downside: disbursed teams could lack a sense of connection and integration. How would new employees become part of the culture? How would difficult conversations take place if the people weren't in the same room? Goodway leaders decided they couldn't leave these important connections to chance. They had to build a framework for making sure that teams stayed united, even across physical distance.

Eric Mossack had already been at Goodway Group for nine years when he got the opportunity to be a part of building this new program. "We call it 'Teams Leading Teams,'" Eric explains, "and the purpose is to give our teams more autonomy to be successful." Eric was hired as the team success partner and began his role providing managers and teams with more resources to develop themselves.

"Having a good relationship with your team can help solve so many problems that organizations face," according to Eric. "If you have a difficult team, no amount of perks like days off or an office ping-pong table can overcome that friction. But if your team has healthy communication, you feel like your voice is being heard, and you can get your problems solved quickly, you're going to enjoy your work more, even when it's hard."

As team success partner, Eric serves in a similar capacity as a business consultant, but a consultant that's internal to the company. He works across the entire organization, functioning as a bridge between management and teams. "We realized that you can't have performance if you don't have cohesiveness, and you can't have cohesiveness if you don't have trust."

So Eric and the team started building trust and serving as a sounding board for leaders and teams to call on. At first, he admits, there was some resistance.

"It can be hard for a group to say, 'There's a problem here. Can you come in and help me fix it?' But once everyone realized that we're on their side, we're not outsiders coming in to point fingers, everyone embraced it. Now, people loop me in all the time! They use me as a resource—even for small things. They'll ping me and ask, 'What should I say to this difficult client?' or 'Hey, I'm having trouble thinking of how to bring up this discussion with my manager.'" Eric's coaching perspective helps both leaders and individual contributors navigate sticky situations. By providing outside input, Eric is seen as a trusted source of guidance to help Goodway employees solve problems and move forward.

With the help of employees like Eric, Goodway Group has seen an increase in their quarterly health monitoring scores. Employees report feeling an increased sense of trust and cohesiveness—inputs that are being actively measured. And now, the Goodway Group is helping nonprofit organizations across the country implement this same framework, increasing their communication and connection.

"This framework helped us stay relevant," Eric says. "In order to achieve our goals, we had to set up our teams to succeed in the new world. That means making sure we're fully connected, even when we're far apart." Goodway Group recognizes that stellar performance relies on cohesiveness and trust. To achieve at peak levels, people must feel a sense of community and be willing to ask for help.

When your drive for success outweighs
your discomfort with vulnerability,
you'll be ready to move forward.

Think about building a snowman as a child: if you invite three friends over to make a snowman, you have four people helping to pick up the middle section and the top section to place them on top of the snowman's body. With four people, you can lift larger sections. With four sets of eyes, you can see the snowman from all angles and make sure all his parts are on straight and not tilting over before you let go. You can build a bigger, better snowman with four people than with one, *and* you can even make sure he's more solid and secure. All because you aren't doing it alone.

If you feel uncomfortable requesting someone else's help, ask yourself this question: *What's more important—that I succeed at this or that I avoid discomfort?* Refusing to ask for help is often a way we allow our ego to take the lead. We're preserving a sense of superiority, a sense of "I can do it myself," but we're doing it at the expense of achieving what we claim to want. Are you really willing to risk not achieving your goals because you won't ask for outside input? Is it better not to solve this problem at all than to solve it using assistance from someone else's wisdom?

When your drive for success outweighs your discomfort with vulnerability, you'll be ready to move forward. So how do you get comfortable with being *un*comfortable? How do you find the confidence to let your vulnerability show? Find a role model who knows that even leaders make mistakes.

The Vulnerability Effect

Ed Catmull doesn't avoid talking about what he's done wrong. He's a man who dwells on his failures, and he encourages everyone around him to dwell on their failures, too. That might sound like an undesirable quality, but his success proves otherwise. Catmull is the cofounder of Pixar and served as president of Disney Animation Studios.

When making a film, Catmull uses a different strategy than many other filmmakers. It's common in the film industry for studio heads to ask themselves, *What worked about the last film?* and attempt to replicate that success. But Catmull thinks that's a losing strategy that leads to similar films getting made over and over again.

Instead, Catmull performs a postmortem on every film his studio finishes. He doesn't just look at what went right; he also explores what went wrong. He and his team pore over the data in search of patterns and clues, trying to piece together even the smallest opportunities for improvement. They focus on the missteps just as much as the successes, regardless of how well the film performed at the box office. And that data allows them to improve over time. Most importantly, Catmull doesn't keep that data to himself. He tells everyone at Disney/Pixar what he discovered. And he uses it to train new hires.

Think about your first day as a new hire at a job. Usually, you're welcomed with an informational packet about the company's background. Some of your team might do a short presentation about the organization's history, core values, mission, and vision. You'll probably learn about the key stakeholders and start getting up to speed on the systems. That's a typical onboarding session at many companies. You talk about the good stuff.

That's not what Ed Catmull does, though. When new hires join Pixar, Catmull has a surprise for them. He shows up—the big boss makes an appearance!—and tells the new staff members stories. Specifically, he tells them stories about failures and mistakes. He doesn't do it to promote a negative atmosphere. Catmull shares stories of mistakes because he believes it's important for new hires to leave their fear of failure at the door. He recognizes that in order to be successful at Pixar, employees need to feel comfortable putting forward ideas, even if those ideas don't work out.

If Ed Catmull, the big boss, can make a mistake and own it, then so can every single employee at Pixar. By sharing stories of failure, Catmull is fostering a culture where his team can share stories and ask for help. They can raise their hand and admit, "I'm stuck," and it isn't something to be embarrassed about; it's just a natural part of the process of taking on something new and uncertain.

Society is changing. No longer do leaders have to hold themselves up as infallible, God-like creatures. Many leaders are beginning to realize the benefits of vulnerability and admitting their mistakes, both to themselves and to others. If you can't find a role model like this in real life, fill yourself with stories like Ed Catmull's. And try being vulnerable first. You may find that when you admit your missteps and ask for help, others around you start opening up, too.

The Magic of Perspective

Have you ever seen one of the optical illusion tricks that are common in children's magazines? When you look at it the first time, you'd swear the image was of one thing, but if you look at it more closely, a different image starts to emerge. Two people could look at the same photo and have two completely different impressions of what's pictured.

Perspective is funny like that: our own perspective feels like the absolute truth to us. It's our reality. But to someone else, the situation could be perceived completely differently. Perspective is the reason for the saying, "There are three sides to every story: his, hers, and the truth." We all see life through our own lens, and sometimes other people's lenses give them an entirely different impression of the same thing. Like in the optical illusion on page 169—if you saw a young woman, you wouldn't be wrong. But if you started to swear that it was *definitely* a young woman and *only* a young woman, the people who see only the old woman would think you're crazy and the people who see both the young woman and the old woman might think you are narrow-minded.

W. E. Hill, "My Wife and My Mother-in-Law."[1]

More perspective pays off.

When someone says they want to "get perspective," that usually means they're trying to put aside their own lens and look through the lenses of others—to see the world from the perspective of someone else, or many other people.

The benefits of perspective go beyond simply understanding and having compassion for another person. Teams that prioritize perspective-sharing tend to have a more cohesive culture, like Goodway Group. And workplaces that encourage the sharing of stories, which build perspective, have been shown to be better positioned to weather change.

Organizations across the world have recently begun realizing how differing perspectives can benefit the bottom line. Many companies launched diversity initiatives as a "politically correct" maneuver, originally hoping that increasing diversity would keep them from running afoul of anti-discrimination laws. But in time, research began to make clear that diversity was more than a politically correct move: organizations with diverse leadership delivered higher profits.[2] More perspective pays off.

Think about it: the more diverse the background of a team, the more diverse the solutions will be that are brought to the table.[3] When individuals share their different experiences and expertise, the group can make better decisions, because they're able to see a problem from more angles.

As an individual, you can still benefit from this strategy. When asking other people for guidance, don't just ask your closest friend, especially if that person is your closest friend because they're similar to you and they just "get" you. Find someone you trust who has a completely different life experience than yours, because they might have a take on the situation that you haven't thought of. And if you ask multiple people for input, seek out people who aren't just different from you but are also different from one another. Compare and contrast their suggestions, and see where you find overlap.

Allowing other people to share their perspectives with you can often feel difficult. Your worldview is a part of who you are, and challenging that worldview with new possibilities can feel uncomfortable. When I conducted my research, I expected to find that older individuals would be less inclined to seek out the perspectives of others, but the results surprised me. When answering the question "I value understanding different perspectives from my own," older employees agreed at the highest levels and younger employees agreed at the lowest levels.[4]

Whatever your age, use input and stories from other people to help guide your path forward. When you "get perspective" by looking at a situation through a new lens, you're broadening your knowledge base and increasing your ability to make smart decisions.

Seeking Out Perspective

When I was recovering from brain surgery, I found perspective in an unexpected place.

I was still healing, spending a lot of my day in bed, while trying to run the Austin Involved nonprofit at the same time. During my first volunteer day back after being cleared by my doctor, I was exhausted but exhilarated. It felt so good to be back doing something "normal." But as we finished our volunteer work that afternoon, I didn't want it to be over. I realized that volunteering was giving me more than just a feeling of normalcy—I was feeling a sense of purpose starting to return.

I looked it up after that day, and I discovered that it's not uncommon for people who volunteer to report an increased sense of perspective. But that perspective doesn't happen for the reasons I assumed. I would have guessed that volunteering gives us something called a "downward comparison"—that's when you consider the experience of someone else and realize your problems aren't as bad as the other person's. You're able to get perspective on your problems because you can recognize that someone else has it worse.

I was surprised to discover that's not the full story: downward comparison isn't why helping someone else allows us get perspective. In fact, it's not about comparison at all. The reason volunteering gives us perspective is because when we help someone else, we realize that we have the ability to effect change. If you've ever participated in a volunteer activity and seen someone's face light up at the help the nonprofit provided, you know how powerful you can feel. You may have just been a part of changing someone's life!

When you provide help to someone else, whether it's through formal volunteering or just person to person, you're also triggering a cognitive process in your brain that reminds you how capable you are—how much power you have to change things. And if you can change circumstances in someone else's life, you can change circumstances in your own.

The next time you NEED help, give help. Experiencing someone else's story will give you perspective on your own story. And it can provide you with the power boost you need to make change.

Pick Up the Red Pen

"Map out your future, but do it in pencil."
—Jon Bon Jovi

*L*ike millions of people, I use a computer for work every day. And I hate it when my computer interrupts me in the middle of what I'm doing to ping me with an alert telling me it's time to download an update. It feels like I'm required to update the operating system every few weeks!

I once managed to avoid downloading the update for months. I kept deleting the reminder on my computer, hiding it away. Out of sight, out of mind. Until the day my computer wouldn't work. I tried the timeless strategy of shutting it off and turning it back on. But it didn't want to reboot. I tried the *next* best approach of calling my husband and making HIM fix it. He took the computer from me and started fiddling with it. Then the noises began:

"Hmmm...HMMMM...oh. Honey, how long has it been since you've updated the operating system?"

"Uh...maybe...a little while...?"

"You can't load any of your programs because they won't run on the old operating system anymore. You're months behind on downloading an update."

To me, it felt easier to skip downloading the update. And for a while, it was easier...until it wasn't.

Like computers, sometimes we must download an update in order to keep running. If we don't update, we become obsolete. We can't perform efficiently. We can't keep up with the new requirements. We can't do what we were designed to do. Downloading an update is a natural part of operating technology, and it's a natural part of operating your life.

What if having to revise your life plan is a blessing instead of a curse?

What if the red pen of revision isn't an ominous sign that you're doing something wrong, but a helpful tool to get you even closer to the goals you've dreamed of reaching?

What if change is a necessary part of *every* success story, including yours?

Within these pages, you've heard stories of people who have walked this path before. You've been given some new tools for increasing your flexibility and resilience when you're called on to adapt. And hopefully, you've had the opportunity to develop a better relationship to change.

As you move forward on your new path, remember that having to alter your course isn't a failure on your part. It's an opportunity you're choosing to take. When life throws you a curveball, it's not because *you* need fixing. It's because your plan needs revising.

As you read these words, you might be facing difficulty or disappointment. Something in your work life or your home life could be challenging you. You may not have everything you want. But you have more than you realize. You have skills and talents. You have friends, family, and outside support. You have wisdom and experience.

And now you also have a new plan for getting where you want to go.

It's time to stop worrying about what happened to you before or what might happen to you tomorrow. You can analyze the past for clues, and you can plan for the future; but the only time you can take action is today. It's time to **Let Go**, **Think Up**, and **Move On**, so you can focus on the success you deserve.

Grab your red pen. Your new ReVision is waiting for you.

Notes

Introduction

1. Courtney Clark, "Adaptive Thinking Research Report" (Social Research Lab at the University of Northern Colorado, Greeley, Colorado, January 22, 2021).

2. M. E. M. Haglund et al., "Psychobiological mechanisms of resilience: relevance to prevention and treatment of stress-related psychopathology," *Development and Psychopathology* 19, no. 3 (2007): 909, doi: 10.1017/S0954579407000430.

3. See Adam L. Alter et al., "Rising to the threat: Reducing stereotype threat by reframing the threat as a challenge," *Journal of Experimental Social Psychology* 46, no. 1 (2010): 166–171 and Michelle R. Tuckey et al., "Hindrances are not threats: advancing the multidimensionality of work stress," *Journal of Occupational Health Psychology* 20, no. 2 (2015): 131–147.

Chapter 1

1. Clark, "Adaptive Thinking Research Report."

2. David Jansson and Steven M. Smith, "Design fixation," *Design Studies* 12, no. 1 (1991): 3–11, doi: 10.1016/0142-694X(91)90003-F.

Chapter 4

1. A. W. W. Schoennauer, *Problem Finding and Problem Solving*. Chicago: Nelson-Hall, 1981.

2. Min Basadur and Bruce Paton, "Using creativity to boost profits in recessionary times—broadening the playing field," *Industrial Management* 35, no. 1 (1993): 14–19.

3. S. M. Rostan, "Problem finding, problem solving, and cognitive controls: An empirical investigation of critically acclaimed productivity," *Creativity Research Journal* 7, no. 2 (1994): 97–110, doi: 10.1080/10400419409534517.

4. R. Reiter-Palmon and J. J. Illies, "Leadership and creativity: Understanding leadership from a creative problem-solving perspective," *The Leadership Quarterly* 15, no. 1 (2004): 55–77, doi: 10.1016/j.leaqua.2003.12.005; T. B. Ward, S. M. Smith, and J. Vaid, "Conceptual Structures and Processes in Creative Thought," in *Creative Thought: An Investigation of Conceptual Structures and Processes*, eds., T. B. Ward, S. M. Smith, and J. Vaid (Washington, DC: American Psychological Association, 1997), 1–27; Alex F. Osborn, *Applied Imagination: Principles and Procedures of Creative Problem-Solving*, 3rd rev. ed. (New York: Scribner, 1979).

Chapter 5

1. Osborn, Applied Imagination.

2. Clark, "Adaptive Thinking Research Report."

Chapter 6

1. Bernard Nijstad et al., "The Dual Pathway to Creativity Model: Creative Ideation as a Function of Flexibility and Persistence," *European Review of Social Psychology* 21, no. 1 (2010): 34–77.

2. Mark A. Runco, "Predicting Children's Creative Performance," *Psychological Reports* 59, no. 3 (1986): 1247–54.

3. Min Basadur, "Managing the Creative Process in Organizations," in *Problem Finding, Problem Solving, and Creativity*, ed. Mark A. Runco (Norwood, NJ: Abex Publishing Company, 1994), 237–68.

Chapter 7

1. Min Basadur and Peter Hausdorf, "Measuring Divergent Thinking Attitudes Related to Creative Problem Solving and Innovation Management," *Creativity Research Journal* 9, no. 1 (1996): 21–32.

2. Kevin E. Joyce, "Lessons for Employers from *Fortune*'s '100 Best,'" *Business Horizons* 46, no. 2 (2003): 77–84.

3. Nakia S. Gordon et al., "Socially-Induced Brain 'Fertilization': Play Promotes Brain Derived Neurotrophic Factor Transcription in the Amygdala and Dorsolateral Frontal Cortex in Juvenile Rats," *Neuroscience Letters* 341, no. 1 (2003): 17–20.

4. Basadur, "Managing the Creative Process."

5. Peter Felsman, Colleen M. Seifert, and Joseph A. Himle, "The Use of Improvisational Theater Training to Reduce Social Anxiety in Adolescents," *The Arts in Psychotherapy* 63 (2019): 111–117.

Chapter 8

1. R. J. Sternberg, "Implicit Theories of Intelligence, Creativity, and Wisdom," *Journal of Personality and Social Psychology* 49, no. 3 (1985): 607–27.

Chapter 9

1. Katherine Ely, Stephen J. Zaccaro and Elizabeth A. Conjar, "Leadership Development: Training Design Strategies for Growing Adaptability in Leaders," in *The Peak Performing Organization* (London: Routledge, 2009), 175–96.

2. Abdolvahab Baghbanian et al., "Adaptive Decision-Making: How Australian Healthcare Managers Decide," *Australian Health Review* 36, no. 1 (2012): 49–56.

3. Ellen Langer, Arthur Blank, and Benzion Chanowitz, "The Mindlessness of Ostensibly Thoughtful Action: The Role of 'Placebic' Information in Interpersonal Interaction," *Journal of Personality and Social Psychology* 36, no. 6 (1978): 635–42.

4. Wendy Joung, Beryl Hesketh, and Andrew Neal, "Using 'War Stories' to Train for Adaptive Performance: Is It Better to Learn from Error or Success?" *Applied Psychology* 55, no. 2 (2006): 282–302. See also R. E. Lucas et al., "Unemployment Alters the Set Point for Life Satisfaction," *Psychological Science* 15, no. 1 (2004): 8–13, https://psycnet.apa.org/doi/10.1111/j.0963-7214.2004.01501002.x and Daniel Kahneman et al., "When More Pain Is Preferred to Less: Adding a Better End," *Psychological Science* 4, no. 6 (1993): 401–05.

Chapter 10

1. "Youngoldwoman.jpg," *Wikimedia Commons*, August 22, 2005, accessed November 10, 2021, https://commons.wiki media.org/wiki/File:Youngoldwoman.jpg. This image is by the British cartoonist W. E. Hill, "My Wife and My Mother-in-Law," *Puck*, November 6, 1915, and is in the public domain.

2. Vivian Hunt, Dennis Layton, and Sara Prince, "Why diversity matters," McKinsey & Company, January 2015, https://www.mckinsey.com/~/media/mckinsey/business%20functions/organization/our%20insights/why%20diversity%20matters/why%20diversity%20matters.pdf.

3. R. Reiter-Palmon, M. D. Mumford, and K. V. Threlfall, "Solving everyday problems creatively: The role of problem construction and personality type," *Creativity Research Journal* 11 (1998): 187–97.

4. Clark, "Adaptive Thinking Research Report."

Acknowledgments

I am eternally grateful to Phillip Alexander, my first crush, for rejecting me after I beat him in the spelling bee. Because of Phillip, I learned that you can lose something you really want and still have an amazing life. (I also learned that boys aren't quite as tough as they seem, but that's a different book.)

This book wouldn't have been possible without the hard work of David Wildasin, my publisher, and Jennifer Janechek, my editor, both of whom believed in the concept of this book and believed in me. Their guidance has shaped everything in these pages, and they've made my work better. Thank you, Dave and Jen, for proving the research in part 3—that our decisions are always better when made in conjunction with guidance from others. Sam Silverstein, I'm so thankful that you trusted me with an introduction to this incredible crew.

I am inspired by many people, especially my friend Lee Moczy-gemba. At age 97, Lee is busy making plans to retire from the business she owns when she hits 100. We'll see if she actually does, or if she'll still be regularly lunching with friends and clients well past her 100th birthday. Lee is passionate about making every day count, and her unyielding energy is contagious. Lee is my living example of never being too old to change your life for the better.

My family has always supported me no matter what my goals are or how they've changed. Not everyone can say that, and I know I'm lucky to have that support. Thank you for always being my loudest cheering section, whatever the arena. A special shout-out to my father,

L. G. Clark, for always teaching me to "do the hard things first." I thought of him often when it came time to sit down and transfer this book from my mind to the page.

To my mastermind group, the women of Coney Island: you are the fuel in my engine. In being both friends and colleagues, we've somehow built something that goes deeper than either friends *or* colleagues—we've built a family. On the days when I don't even trust myself to make the right decision, I trust you. Coney Island is my happy place, yes, but also my sad place, my hopeful place, my frustrated place, my determined place. In every moment, you make me better at what we do.

To my clients: I am grateful for the trust you have put in me over these past several years. Thank you for allowing me to come in and provide new ways of thinking about change and adaptability, especially during the COVID-19 pandemic.

And to you, the reader: Thank you for believing that you can change for the better. And thank you for taking me on the journey with you.

About the Author

With two successful businesses and four rounds of cancer (so far!) under her belt, Courtney Clark is the luckiest unlucky person in the world.

Diagnosed with cancer for the first time at age 26, Courtney went to work for several cancer nonprofits. At age 29, Courtney founded the nonprofit Austin Involved, creating programs to engage young professionals in philanthropy in simple, affordable ways. In the first year of operating Austin Involved, Courtney was diagnosed with a brain aneurysm and underwent three brain surgeries.

Today, Courtney is an in-demand keynote speaker who presents internationally to organizations on how to adapt faster and achieve more by developing resilience, adaptability and ReVisionary Thinking™. In 2021, Courtney became a Certified Speaking Professional™, a designation earned by only 17 percent of speakers worldwide.

Organizations hire Courtney to speak at their conferences and events because of her unique blend of what she calls "content-based motivation." Her presentations balance left brain strategies with right brain storytelling, so every single member of the audience walks away feeling primed for success, no matter their personality or learning style. She works with teams who need to succeed during stress and change without burning out, lashing out, or giving up.

Courtney's resilience work has been featured in *Forbes*, *Psychology Today*, *USA Today*, and *The Chicago Tribune*. Her first two books, *The Giving Prescription* and *The Successful Struggle*, have been called "practical," "powerful," and "empowering" by industry leaders.

In her free time, Courtney serves on several nonprofit committees and boards of directors. She has been recognized with the Leadership Austin Ascendant Award, the Austin Under 40 Award, and her high school's Distinguished Alumnae Award. She has been recognized by *Austin Monthly* magazine as one of "20 in their 30s," and by *GivingCity* magazine as one of 2012's "New Philanthropists." She has her master's degree in philanthropy from Saint Mary's University of Minnesota, where her graduate research focused on the role of philanthropy in helping people heal from traumatic life events. Her research, which became the basis of her first book, was honored with the University's Outstanding Graduate Research Award.

Courtney's experience in the community has also helped her grow her family. Soon after launching Austin Involved, Courtney and her husband, Jamie, were at an Austin Involved volunteer day when they met a young high school student with dreams of college and success as a musician. Today, Courtney and Jamie have welcomed Anthony into their family, and Courtney can often be seen proudly wearing her "UNT Mom" T-shirt around town. Courtney and her family live in Austin, TX, with so many rescue animals that they have lost count.

Connect with Courtney

Need more from Courtney?

Get even more up-to-date research and strategies
by connecting on social media.

https://www.facebook.com/CourtneyClarkSpeaker

https://twitter.com/courtney_lclark (that's an "L" like "lemon")

https://www.linkedin.com/in/courtneylclark/

https://www.youtube.com/c/CourtneyLClark

Interested in bringing Courtney in to speak to your group?

Courtney loves working with teams to create high-energy,
interactive presentations on resilience and adaptability.

To learn more about bringing her to your conference or event, scan
the QR code below or visit http://www.courtneyclark.com/speaking.

Do you have a story of ReVision you want to share?

Courtney is still collecting stories to help others,
and she'd love to hear from you:

https://www.courtneyclark.com/stories/

UPGRADE YOUR LIBRARY WITH
DOZENS OF CLASSIC BOOKS FROM
BEST-SELLING AUTHORS LIKE...

NAPOLEON HILL

ZIG ZIGLAR

EARL NIGHTINGALE

CAVETT ROBERT

GEORGE S. CLASON

W. CLEMENT STONE

AND MANY MORE!

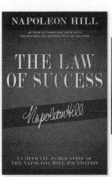

CLAIM YOUR ADDITIONAL

FREE BOOKS & RESOURCES:

WWW.SOUNDWISDOM.COM/CLASSICS